Advance Praise for

TAX STRATEGIES
FOR EVERYONE

"Capitalism aims to benefit society through self-interest. The US government designed our tax code on the same ideal: Reward taxpayers for providing value to society. Tax expert Eric Freeman offers a refreshing and easy-to-understand path that preserves our self-interest as taxpayers with money-saving methods, while leveraging our government's desire to serve the greater good. I highly recommend it!"

—**DAN J. SANDERS,** New York Times *and* USA Today *bestselling author and former COO, Sprouts Farmers Market*

. . .

"Whether you're an employee, retiree, self-employed, or business owner, *Tax Strategies for Everyone* makes the complex world of taxes understandable. By outlining the key principles and tenets of taxation, Eric Freeman provides the tips and insight you'll need to make informed decisions, mitigate your tax burden, and leverage opportunities on your journey to financial success."

—**ERIC MAJCHRZAK,** *CEO, public accounting firm BeachFleischman*

. . .

"As a business owner, a critical part of success is keeping your costs low. Taxes are no exception. Eric Freeman found a way to simplify complex tax concepts with this easy-to-read book. Critical reading for any business owner!"

—**SAM FOX**, *founder, Fox Restaurant Concepts*

"Albert Einstein once said, 'The hardest thing to understand in the world is the income tax,' and there's probably some truth to that. However, Eric Freeman does a nice job of breaking down complex concepts into explanations that the typical taxpayer can comprehend. Furthermore, *Tax Strategies for Everyone* doesn't need to be read cover to cover; readers can pick and choose which chapters are relevant to them. Two thumbs up to this guide."

—**THOMAS KLEIN,** *CPA, Distinguished Teaching Professor, University of Arizona*

· · ·

"*Tax Strategies for Everyone* isn't a textbook. It's too well-writen, witty and engaging. Author and CPA Eric Freeman has produced a real estate wealth-building guide that is filled with practical advice and investment strategies that anyone can follow to start building their own real estate empire. Valuable advice indeed!"

—**GEORGE LARSEN,** *founder, Larsen Baker, LLC*

TAX
STRATEGIES
FOR
EVERYONE

...

HOW TO SLASH YOUR TAXES
AND BUILD WEALTH

ERIC FREEMAN, CPA, MAcc

ERIC FREEMAN, CPA, MAcc   Vol. 1

TAX STRATEGIES

FOR
EVERYONE

HOW TO SLASH YOUR TAXES
AND BUILD WEALTH

KM PRESS

Phoenix, Arizona

Published by KM Press

KM Press
15170 N. Hayden Road
Scottsdale, AZ 85260
480-998-5400

Learn more at: www.kenmcelroy.com

ISBN: 979-8-9895781-0-8 (Print)
ISBN: 979-8-9895781-1-5 (E-Readers)

Printed in the United States of America

RICH FETTKE

The Wise Investor
A Modern Parable About Creating Financial Freedom and Living Your Best Life

MIKE MALONEY

Guide to Investing in Gold & Silver
Protect Your Financial Future

STRATEGIES SERIES

Branding and Marketing Strategies for Everyone

Real Estate Strategies for Everyone

Legal Strategies for Everyone

Sales Strategies for Everyone

Tax Strategies for Everyone

ABCs of Raising Capital
Only Lazy People Use Their Own Money

Speak and Get What You Want
Communicate Like the World's Most Successful Leaders

TABLE OF CONTENTS

INTRODUCTION:
IT DEPENDS

If you're like most people, you'd rather talk to a wall than deal with your taxes. I'll admit it, even for a CPA, taxes can be tedious. But taxes are likely the biggest expense of your lifetime, so you must pay attention to them if you're going to run a successful business or achieve any level of financial success.

There's a great scene from the TV series *Parks and Recreation* where the character Ron Swanson is explaining how government works to a young girl named Lauren. In the final seconds of the scene, Ron takes a large bite of the girl's sandwich and says, "and I get to take 40 percent of your lunch, and that, Lauren, is how taxes work."

It's a great illustration of how taxes work, but, in my opinion, Ron did not take a big enough bite. Realistically, far more than 40 percent of what you earn may be eaten up by taxes, when you consider not only **federal income taxes,** but **state income taxes, sales taxes, self-employment taxes, property taxes,** and more.

I don't know about you, but I treasure my lunch and want to eat all of it! Or at least as much as possible. My goal for writing this book is to supply you with a basic working knowledge of federal income taxes so you can legally and ethically reduce the biggest expense of your lifetime.

I'm not saying learning about taxes is as entertaining as watching a sitcom or as simple as a Ron Swanson analogy. However, I think this book will help you learn how to keep more money in your pocket as you work toward your financial goals—and that should sound like fun!

I like to tell my colleagues, "If you're not miserable, you're not learning." It only takes one unexpectedly large tax bill to make you miserable enough to make you want to learn more about taxes. If you're reading this book, you've likely felt that misery. Now it's time to learn how to avoid it.

As I've mentioned, there are many forms of taxes, but this book will focus on federal income taxes. That's where your biggest tax bills are likely to come, and getting a handle on federal taxes will likely give you a head start on dealing with state and local taxes, too. Many states follow federal tax laws in establishing their income taxes, although they use different tax rates or modify the **tax base.** Throughout the book, I may mention some differences you are likely to find in state income taxes, but the focus of the book is on federal taxes. So, just assume I am discussing federal income taxes unless I say otherwise.

The tax laws are constantly changing, likely more often than the average taxpayer imagines. In fact, there are often new laws that come into play in the middle of a tax year or even laws passed after year end and made retroactive to a previous tax year. Many of the limitations, thresholds, tax brackets, mileage rates, and more have built-in annual adjustments for inflation or may pick up or drop off in specific tax years. At any time there could also be a tax court case, guidance from the IRS or other interpretation that changes the implementation of current laws. However, large tax code over-hauls historically come decades apart. The last major overhaul was in 2017, and before that it was in 1986 and 1954. I've written the book with examples and numbers from the 2024 tax year. Many of these are not slated to change, but others will be adjusted annually with inflation or change for other reasons.

Many say a picture is worth a thousand words. A number is the equivalent of a picture in the tax world. For that reason, I felt it prudent to use current numbers to illustrate points and give you a good idea of how to use the strategies in this book to your advantage. You'll be able to find updated amounts easily online and should certainly check, even if it's for the 2024 tax year as anything could change at any time. Visit my website TaxStrategiesForEveryone.com for current tax updates and annual changes.

Using This Book

The tax code is extremely nuanced, and this book cannot give you personalized advice about your specific situation because the same answer does not apply in all circumstances. In one case something may be *taxable income*, while, in another situation, it may not be.

When my clients ask me whether something is deductible or whether a certain tax will apply to their business, my answer is often, "It depends." They've heard that response so frequently that they will often answer my questions that way. They do it jokingly—I hope.

Frustrating as it may be to hear "it depends" when you ask a tax question, it's also the reality. When you're dealing with federal taxes, it almost always depends. It depends on the details of your business. It depends on your income goals. It depends on how you have invested your money. It depends on how you have structured your business. It depends on where you live and how many **employees** you have. It depends on what changes the government has made to the tax code that year or how the courts have interpreted a new law. The list is endless.

So, if there are so many specific variables when dealing with taxes, can reading a book like this even help you?

Yes. Because when you understand basic tax concepts, you will realize that even small changes in the way you do business can have a huge impact on your tax bill. This book will help you understand those general concepts so you can recognize which information is relevant to your situation and know which questions to ask and when to ask them. When you can do that, you'll be ready to help a competent tax advisor keep you from paying more than your fair share of taxes. And this book can even help you find a competent tax advisor! (See Chapter 13.)

....

A Tractor for Christmas?

I once had a client ask me whether he should rush to purchase a utility tractor before the end of the year to help reduce his taxes. He wasn't going to need to use the tractor before the end of the year, but he knew he would need it at some point during the next year when he would be grading and building a new home as part of his real estate portfolio.

My initial reply was, "Well, it depends."

Then I asked my client a few more questions to figure out how his income in the current year would compare with what he was likely to make in the next year. I discovered there wasn't much income in the current year to offset. And we determined that purchasing the tractor in the current year could actually trigger some tax limitations.

From all predictions, it appeared that my client would be in a much better tax position if he made the tractor purchase in the next year. This conversation helped my client with his cash flow management and prevented him from making a big tax mistake.

Had the situation been different, I might have told him to do everything he could to buy that tractor as soon as possible.

It depends. It always depends.

....

Keeping It Simple

To help explain a complex topic, I've included tip boxes throughout the book with easy-to-understand information and advice. These boxes will help illustrate information in the text and give you additional material to ponder. Scattered throughout the book, you will find these five varieties of tip boxes:

STRATEGY TIP

When you have a basic understanding of a concept, you should start to develop a strategy for minimizing your tax burden. Read these tips to help you get started.

BEWARE

Avoid potential pitfalls and don't fall for common tax traps.

TAX TENETS

Incorporate these philosophies in your mindset to maximize tax savings.

IT GOES HERE

Discover where to indicate specific income and deductions in the IRS tax forms.

IN CASE OF AUDIT

Learn what to do—and not to do—if the IRS singles you out for an audit.

You will also discover sidebars that illustrate how taxes can affect the lives of real people, and chapter summaries that offer the main points of each chapter. And at the end of the book, you will find a glossary that provides definitions of important or confusing (and sometimes important *and* confusing) terms and concepts discussed throughout the book.

Despite the complexity and nuances of tax law, the information provided in the following chapters will give you a solid foundation to start analyzing your own tax situation. The strategy tips and tax planning ideas in this book will help you establish your own tax philosophy and introduce some tactics you can employ to lower your tax bill.

Although the book will help you know which questions to ask, you should still plan to talk with a qualified tax advisor before implementing any specific strategies. There are too many exceptions and nuances for me to address all of the factors that could apply to you—especially without meeting you or knowing details about you or your business.

If you're not already working with a qualified tax advisor, make sure you take special note of the tips in Chapter 13 to help you find the best tax advisor for you and your situation.

TAX TENET #1
It always depends.

1

TAX SAVINGS HIDE
ABOVE THE LINE

The main purpose of taxes is to provide value for society. The government uses revenue from taxes to pay for goods and services that it perceives as important for society. The reality is there are certain goods and services a society needs as a collective to flourish. If you weren't forced to, would you pay taxes so the roads in your city could be paved? If you would pay for the roads, would your neighbor?

Now, what should a government value? And how much should it tax its citizens to pay for what it values? These are the questions at the heart of most political conflicts. We're not looking at these questions in this book; we are just dealing with the underlying principles of taxation and the U.S. tax code.

But here's an important underlying principle that you may not understand as well: the greater the value provided by you or your business, the less you can pay in taxes.

If what you produce does not provide enough collective value, the government will take your money and provide value on your behalf. The government will use your money to provide goods and services it perceives as important for society.

But when the government perceives that you are providing value for society, it will allow you to keep more of your money.

If you view the tax code in the simple formula of Greater Value = Lower Taxes, you will more easily grasp the nuances of the federal tax code. You don't need to be a tax guru to take advantage of the tax system—you just need to figure out how to show that you are producing value to society.

The tax code itself is over 7,000 pages long, but this doesn't even come close to describing how complex the code can be. In addition to the thousands of pages of code, there are regulations, notices, court cases, and many other forms of guidance. But you don't have to read all those documents to understand the most important tax principle. All you need to remember is that tax law is a collective of rules that explains what a government values. (Hopefully what the government values aligns with what society values. But again, that's a question for a different book.)

Ways To Create Tax-Lowering Value

There are almost endless opportunities for businesses and individuals to create value in the government's eyes. Setting up retirement plans for your employees will often generate tax benefits for both the employer and the employees because you are reducing some of the government's burden for supporting these individuals in retirement.

Businesses often receive more tax benefits than individuals because the government views actions taken by businesses as providing more value to society. This principle will become evident throughout the book as we discuss the many common **deductions** and lower tax rates given to businesses. For example, when you employ multiple people in your business there is a reduction in self-employment taxes. The government values job creation and will reap a return in lowering the business owner's employment taxes by collecting more employment taxes from the employees themselves.

Both individuals and businesses can glean massive tax benefits from owning and investing in real estate. Real estate is important to society regardless of your position. Real estate provides everything from a roof over our heads to a place to manufacture critical goods; that's why the government wants to incentivize investment in real estate: it's good for everyone. We will dive into this subject more in Chapter 10 when I cover real estate taxes in detail.

These are only a few examples of how anyone can create value and therefore lower their taxes. Pay extra attention to the Strategy Tips sprinkled throughout the book to get additional information on finding tax benefits.

TAX TENET #2

The greater the value you provide, the less you will pay in taxes.

Let's Look at the Basics

To understand how you are taxed, let's start with how taxes are organized. This is the basic formula:

> *Gross Income*
> – *Above the Line Deductions*
> = ***Adjusted Gross Income***
>
> *Adjusted Gross Income*
> – *Standard or Itemized Deductions*
> = ***Taxable Income***

Let's define these terms. **Gross income** is easy to understand because the government says all income is included (unless it's not). Gross income includes what you earn as an employee or as a business owner. This also includes any ***personal income.*** Personal income would come from items not considered part of your job or your business. For example, if you sell your home, the income from the sale would be part of your gross income. Later we'll talk about an exception to this rule. You need to pay attention to the exceptions because exceptions are the government telling you when you've created value.

Deductions from your gross income are expenses the government allows you to deduct to arrive at your taxable income. No expense is a tax deduction unless the government tells you it is. While personal income is almost always included in gross income, personal expenses rarely create tax deductions. A great way to reduce your overall tax bill is to find ways to convert personal expenses into deductible expenses. You do that by showing how your personal expenses create collective value. I'll give you ideas for doing this in Chapter 8.

Your **adjusted gross income** (AGI) is a defining line on the tax return. A tax professional will often mention the difference between **above the line deductions** and **below the line deductions.** AGI is the dividing "line." Deductions that are literally positioned above the AGI line on a tax return directly affect your AGI. Any deductions that are below your AGI line are standard or itemized deductions, which will lower your tax bill but not as much as above the line deductions.

IT GOES HERE

Individuals calculate their taxes on Form 1040. On this form you will see the basic tax formula.

Above the Line vs. Below the Line

It's important to understand the difference between above and below the line deductions because above the line deductions are much more valuable. To really understand this concept, you must know what is meant by a **standard deduction** and an **itemized deduction**. Both of these are below the line deductions.

Every individual taxpayer is entitled to either a standard deduction or itemized deductions. You can't have your cake and eat it too, so you need to pick which one you will take. Obviously, you would rather have more deductions to reduce your tax burden, so you will choose the option that gives you the largest deduction possible.

The standard deduction is a specific dollar amount determined by your filing status. This is what I'd refer to as a "freebie." You can take the standard deduction against your income regardless of what actual deductions you may have. In other words, it's not tied to any inflows or outflows of cash you may have. The standard deduction is adjusted for inflation each year. You can easily find the current standard deduction amounts online each year as they are typically released by the IRS around late fall for the next tax year. You can also check my website, TaxStrategiesForEveryone.com, for these updates. Table 1.1 shows the standard deduction amounts by filing status for the tax year 2024. We'll cover more about filing statuses in Chapter 2.

Table 1.1. Standard deduction amounts

Filing Status	Standard Deduction
Single; married filing separately	$14,600
Married filing jointly; surviving spouses	$29,200
Head of household	$21,900

You can think of itemized deductions as expenses or as cash outflows that are personal in nature—not tied to a business. Of course, this doesn't mean you're allowed a tax deduction for every personal expense you have. Only certain personal expenses can be taken as an itemized deduction, and many of them will be subject to their own specific limitation. The most common expenses allowed as itemized deductions are listed below.

IT GOES HERE

Itemized deductions are reported on Schedule A.

MEDICAL EXPENSES

This can include health insurance, doctors, dentists, hospitals, eye exams, and even transportation costs associated with these expenses. But don't worry too much about using these as an itemized deduction unless you have a significant amount because medical expenses are severely limited as a tax deduction. You can only deduct the amount of medical expenses that exceed 7.5 percent of your AGI. If you know your medical expenses won't be greater than that amount, don't worry about tracking them. It will be wasted effort.

IN CASE OF AUDIT

In the event you take a deduction for medical expenses, make sure to keep all your receipts to substantiate the amounts. Unlike some other items of income or deduction, these are not reported to the IRS. It will be your responsibility to prove the expenses.

MORTGAGE INTEREST

This is typically the largest itemized deduction for most taxpayers. Mortgage *interest* is only an itemized deduction when it's for your principal residence or a second home. Not only are you limited to two homes, but your interest deduction is limited to a total debt of $750,000 or less. Unlike many other items in the tax code, this number is not adjusted for inflation each year. In fact, this number has actually decreased! Prior to 2018, you were able to deduct interest expense on up to $1 million. Now any debt that you had prior to the law change would be grandfathered in. As the cost of housing rises, this deduction becomes less and less useful.

STRATEGY TIP

Mortgage interest won't be limited as an itemized deduction if it is interest on a rental property you own or for a building that you use in your business.

IN CASE OF AUDIT

Home mortgage interest is reported on Form 1098 by your bank at the end of each year, and a copy is sent to you and the IRS. The IRS will match the 1098 received with what you report on your tax return. This does not mean you will automatically get the deduction if you don't report it. But there may be an issue if you report a different amount from what your mortgage lender reports.

INVESTMENT INTEREST

Investment interest for most would be margin interest on a stock portfolio. However, this could be interest expense on any type of investment but would not include any interest expense on consumer debt such as interest associated with the purchase of a family vehicle or personal credit cards. It would also not include interest expense that is already characterized as deductible somewhere else on the tax return, such as interest expense on rental real estate and interest expense associated with running a business. If the interest expense is not related to a consumer debt, rental real estate, or a business, then it is likely investment interest expense.

BEWARE

Investment interest from debt used to generate tax-exempt income is not deductible. Many times this debt will be from investing in tax-exempt municipal bonds.

IN CASE OF AUDIT

Brokerages are required to send you a Consolidated Form 1099 shortly after the end of each tax year if you have any reportable transactions. Most will include investment interest paid. This amount is not typically reported to the IRS like most of the other transactions on this form. Make sure to keep a copy of Form 1099 and use it when deducting your investment interest.

Let's not get too excited about this deduction. Like the other itemized deductions, it has its own limitations. You can only deduct investment interest expense to the extent you have net investment income. Investment income will generally include interest, **dividends, annuities,** and **royalties.** If you don't have any investment income, then your investment interest expense won't be allowed as a deduction. There is a silver lining, though: any investment interest expense that is not deductible can be used in a future tax year when you do have investment income.

STRATEGY TIP

While capital gain from the sale of stock and other investments is generally not considered investment income, you can elect to treat it as such. Making this election will increase your investment income for purposes of deducting investment interest expenses. But doing this prevents capital gains from being eligible for their preferential rates. Do the math, or better yet, have your CPA do the math, to see if this election makes sense in any given year.

TAXES

You can deduct personal taxes, such as state income tax, real estate tax, vehicle license taxes, and sales tax. Once again, as you've probably already guessed, there's a limit. Only the first $10,000 of personal taxes are deductible. You must add all the deductible taxes together and anything you paid above this limit will not be deductible on your federal income tax.

STRATEGY TIP

Taxes on investment real estate are not subject to the $10,000 limitation.

IN CASE OF AUDIT

If you have a mortgage on your home, the real estate taxes are typically reported on the same Form 1098 where the mortgage interest is shown. You can reference this easily to determine this portion of your deduction. For any properties without a loan, keep your tax receipts or visit your county treasurer's website to determine the amounts you paid.

CHARITABLE DONATIONS

This deduction is for those who truly want to give. As you'll learn later, deductions only reduce your tax cost; they do not completely offset it. So never give to a nonprofit just to get a tax deduction. Give because it's what you want to do. Charitable donations are generally limited to 60 percent of your AGI. The average taxpayer won't be limited by this alone, but remember, you still don't receive a benefit from your charitable donations unless you itemize your deductions.

I can already imagine someone getting creative with this and claiming a charitable purpose for almost anything. However, to receive the deduction, you must give to an IRS designated nonprofit —which will typically be a 501(c)(3) entity. This is an entity that has applied for tax-exempt status with the IRS and received approval for their charitable purpose. If you plan to itemize a charitable deduction, make sure the organization you give to has this designation.

IN CASE OF AUDIT

Any charitable donation of $250 or more requires a written acknowledgment from the organization in order for you to list your donation as a deduction.

STRATEGY TIP

You can convert charitable contributions into above the line deductions by using a Qualified Charitable Donation (QCD). This is allowed for direct contributions from certain retirement accounts to charitable organizations for taxpayers age 70 1/2 or older.

Once you've determined whether you are entitled to any of these itemized deductions, you total them up, calculate the limitation for each, and add those totals together. This is the itemized deduction available to you. Now compare your itemized deduction total to the standard itemized deduction based on your filing status. If your itemized deductions are greater than the standardized deduction, you should itemize. If your standard deduction is greater, then just take that deduction and ignore the itemized list. If you're like most taxpayers, you'll find the standard deduction is typically higher. The government puts a low value on itemized deductions, which are personal in nature.

Staying above the Line

To get meaningful tax breaks, you must create deductions that are above the line. These are the expenses that the government incentivizes you to incur because they create value.

I hope it's clear that below the line deductions are not the most beneficial to you. The question then becomes, "Can I convert some of my below the line deductions into above the line deductions?"

If you're expecting that I'm going to answer "it depends," then I'm already doing my job. That's exactly right. "It depends."

Although I can't tell you the specifics for your situation, I can tell you that there is a way to move almost every itemized deduction to another section of the tax return. Many of the strategies that make these deductions more beneficial require business, rental, or investment activity, but there are strategies that will benefit employees in addition to business owners.

TAX TENET #3

With the right mindset and good tax planning, every itemized deduction has the potential to be converted into an above the line deduction.

In fact, with the current gig economy and endless ways to generate additional income, converting itemized deductions to above the line deductions has never been easier.

I know I just told you to avoid itemized below the line deductions, but it's important to understand these deductions to understand what actions you can take that will bring you more benefit.

To become an expert in lowering your tax bill, you must build on the basics. You wouldn't add more weight to the barbell before learning the correct form for lifting without hurting yourself, would you? The people who add weight before learning proper form are the ones who are likely to injure themselves before they see progress.

It's no different with taxes. If you try to skip straight into the biggest tax-saving steps without learning the basics, you're likely to wind up in a lot of pain. Learning proper form in weight lifting may not be fun, and learning about itemized deductions is no party, but it's necessary to see gains and minimize taxes.

Chapter Summary

✓ *The greater the value you provide, the less you can pay in taxes.*

✓ *Deductions before AGI are above the line, and deductions after AGI are below the line.*

✓ *Above the line deductions are more beneficial than below the line deductions.*

✓ *Every individual can either take the standard deduction or itemize their deductions, but you can't take both.*

✓ *You can reduce your tax burden by converting itemized, or below the line deductions, into above the line deductions.*

2

NAVIGATING THE PROGRESSIVE TAX MAZE

Two overarching items determine your tax amount: your filing status and your tax bracket, and your tax bracket depends in part on your filing status. As we examine these two building blocks of the U.S. federal tax system, you will notice that as income increases, regardless of filing status, the rate of tax will increase. That is because the United States has a progressive tax system—meaning, the more income you make, the higher percentage of income you pay in taxes.

TAX TENET #4

U.S. federal taxes are progressive.

Although one of the basic tenets of the U.S. tax system is the more money you make, the more tax you pay, there are many ways to reduce your taxable income and/or your tax liability. The most profitable actions don't reduce your overall **economic income.** This is where the idea of value creation becomes most important.

Filing Status

The first stop in determining your tax brackets and therefore the amount of tax you owe will be figuring out your filing status, which will be one of the following:

- Qualifying Surviving Spouse
- Married Filing Jointly
- Head of Household
- Single
- Married Filing Separately

Your filing status is determined by your life status on the last day of the tax year. This list is arranged from the status that will typically result in the lowest tax rates to those that will result in the highest. The tax tables that follow are referred to as your ordinary tax rates, and most income will be subject to **ordinary income** tax rates. Later in the book, we will discuss income that may be eligible for lower tax rates. For now, let's take a closer look at the types of filing status.

The tax tables that follow, which are based on filing status, will change each year with inflation and may change by other acts of law. Remember, you can stay updated on current tax rates by visiting TaxStrategiesForEveryone.com.

QUALIFYING SURVIVING SPOUSE

In the year of your spouse's death, you can file as Married Filing Jointly. For the two years following, you can file as a Qualifying Surviving Spouse. But to qualify for this filing status, you must have a dependent child or stepchild. And the child must have lived in your home for all of the tax year, and you must have paid over half the cost of keeping up your home. Table 2.1 lists the tax brackets for a qualifying surviving spouse for 2024.

Table 2.1. Qualifying surviving spouse

If taxable income is over:	But not over:	The tax is:
$0	$23,200	10 percent of the amount over $0
$23,200	$94,300	$2,320 plus 12 percent of the amount over $23,200
$94,300	$201,050	$10,852 plus 22 percent of the amount over $94,300
$201,050	$383,900	$34,337 plus 24 percent of the amount over $201,050
$383,900	$487,450	$78,221 plus 32 percent of the amount over $383,900
$457,450	$731,200	$111,357 plus 35 percent of the amount over $487,450
$731,200	No limit	$196,669.50 plus 37 percent of the amount over $731,200

MARRIED FILING JOINTLY

This filing status is reserved for married couples. Filing under this status means that all the income and deductions for each spouse are included on a single tax return. The tax rates are applied to all the income of the couple combined. Table 2.2 shows the tax brackets for Married Filing Jointly for 2024.

Table 2.2. Married filing jointly

If taxable income is over:	But not over:	The tax is:
$0	$23,200	10 percent of the amount over $0
$23,200	$94,300	$2,320 plus 12 percent of the amount over $23,200
$94,300	$201,050	$10,852 plus 22 percent of the amount over $94,300
$201,050	$383,900	$34,337 plus 24 percent of the amount over $201,050
$383,900	$487,450	$78,221 plus 32 percent of the amount over $383,900
$457,450	$731,200	$111,357 plus 35 percent of the amount over $487,450
$731,200	No limit	$196,669.50 plus 37 percent of the amount over $731,200

The most significant benefit of filing Married Filing Jointly is that it takes twice as much income to reach the same tax bracket as a single taxpayer. You might think this is common sense so what's the benefit? The benefit is that it's rare for both spouses to make exactly the same amount of income.

For example, assume one spouse is making $80,000 annually and the other spouse is a homemaker with no income. If the spouse making $80,000 annually was a single filer, they would be in the 22 percent tax bracket. But when Married Filing Jointly, that same taxpayer is only in the 12 percent tax bracket. Without running through the numbers, it's already obvious that the spouse with income is paying a fraction of the tax as they would if they were to file Single, or even Married Filing Separately. As a collective, the couple has a much lower tax burden by utilizing this tax benefit. This will be the case any time one spouse has more income than another spouse. It should also be noted that the standard deduction for married filing joint taxpayers is twice that of a single taxpayer, as you learned in Chapter 1. This can further reduce a married couple's tax burden.

STRATEGY TIP

Choosing whether to get married at the end of a tax year or the beginning of the next tax year can make a dramatic difference in the taxes you pay. Since your filing status is based on the last day of the tax year, you may lower your taxes by marrying before the end of the year.

TAX TENET #5

Marriage affects your taxes, but don't get married for lower taxes.

HEAD OF HOUSEHOLD

The Head of Household filing status is generally for unmarried taxpayers who provide a home for themselves and a dependent. In this status, you receive wider tax brackets than a Single filer or Married Filing Separately. Table 2.3 shows tax brackets for Head of Household for 2024.

Table 2.3. Head of household

If taxable income is over:	But not over:	The tax is:
$0	$16,550	10 percent of the amount over $0
$16,550	$63,100	$1,655 plus 12 percent of the amount over $16,550
$63,100	$100,500	$7,241 plus 22 percent of the amount over $63,100
$100,500	$191,950	$15,469 plus 24 percent of the amount over $100,500
$191,950	$243,700	$37,417 plus 32 percent of the amount over $191,950
$243,700	$609,350	$53,977 plus 35 percent of the amount over $243,700
$609,350	no limit	$181,954.50 plus 37 percent of the amount over $609,350

STRATEGY TIP

There are times you can use Head of Household status to your benefit even if you are legally married. This applies if you were legally separated or if you lived apart from your spouse for at least six months and paid over half the cost of keeping up your home for a child, stepchild, or foster child for more than half the year.

SINGLE

This filing status is reserved for those taxpayers who are not married and do not qualify as either Head of Household or Qualifying Surviving Spouse. Table 2.4 shows tax brackets for Single filers for 2024.

Table 2.4. Single

If taxable income is over:	But not over:	The tax is:
$0	$11,600	10 percent of the amount over $0
$11,600	$47,150	$1,160 plus 12 percent of the amount over $11,600
$47,150	$100,525	$5,426 plus 22 percent of the amount over $47,150
$100,525	$191,950	$17,168.50 plus 24 percent of the amount over $100,525
$191,950	$243,725	$39,110.50 plus 32 percent of the amount over $191,950
$243,725	$609,350	$55,678.50 plus 35 percent of the amount over $243,725
$609,350	no limit	$183,647.25 plus 37 percent of the amount over $609,350

MARRIED FILING SEPARATELY

As you might imagine, this filing status is for those who are married but choose not to file a joint tax return. This is usually the least beneficial filing status and therefore usually reserved for married couples who are separated. There may be other reasons for using this status, but they are almost never tax related. I've heard of some attorneys recommending this filing status for a spouse who wants to keep distance from any potential legal issues that may arise from their partner's businesses or other assets. Check with an attorney in your state for whether this may have any validity if it's a concern. Table 2.5 shows tax brackets for Married Filing Separately for 2024.

Table 2.5. Married filing separately

If taxable income is over:	But not over:	The tax is:
$0	$11,600	10 percent of the amount over $0
$11,600	$47,150	$1,160 plus 12 percent of the amount over $11,600
$47,150	$100,525	$5,426 plus 22 percent of the amount over $47,150
$100,525	$191,950	$17,168.50 plus 24 percent of the amount over $100,525
$191,950	$243,725	$39,110.50 plus 32 percent of the amount over $191,950
$243,725	$365,600	$55,678.50 plus 35 percent of the amount over $243,725
$365,600	no limit	$98,334.75 plus 37 percent of the amount over $365,600

Like the standard deduction amounts covered in Chapter 1, these tax tables are adjusted for inflation each year. These will typically be released by the IRS in the late fall. While these tables and potentially the rates will change each year, it's important to study these as part of your understanding on how your income will be taxed. I will also build on these tables to further illustrate points as we move through the chapter.

IN CASE OF AUDIT

The higher your income, the more likely you are to be audited by the IRS. The reason makes sense. There are larger numbers involved and therefore finding errors on the return is more likely to be worth the effort. Higher income tax returns also tend to be more complex by nature and are therefore more prone to have potential adjustments for the IRS to find.

Marginal Tax Brackets

If your friend says, "I'm in the 24 percent *marginal tax bracket,*" do you know what that means?

Before you read this book, you might have believed your friend was talking about the percentage of tax he is actually paying. But pay attention now and you will be able to correct your mistake. And maybe even correct someone else at the next dinner party.

The marginal tax rate means the highest tax rate someone will pay on their income. Of course, you also know that a person's tax bracket is related to income and filing status.

....

Illustrating the Marginal Tax Rate

Jason has a taxable income of $110,000 and files Single. Looking at Table 2.4, you see that $110,000 falls in the 24 percent tax bracket. However, only the income above $100,525—or $9,475—will be taxed at 24 percent. That means Jason's marginal tax rate is 24 percent. A person's marginal tax rate identifies more about their income than the actual tax rate they are paying on that income. So, knowing your marginal tax rate gives you very little insight into how much the tax man is actually taking from your hard earned income.

....

Many people believe when their income pushes them into a higher tax bracket all their income will be taxed at the higher rate. Of course, you will not fall victim to this false belief. At least, you won't believe it anymore. Not since you were smart enough to read this book.

Because now you know that when your income increases enough to reach the next tax bracket, only the additional income is subject to the higher rate. This is your marginal tax rate. The income in each of the brackets below remains subject to those lower rates. Therefore, it is always better to make more income, regardless of the higher tax rate. You will end up with more after-tax dollars with more income, despite a higher rate applied to that income.

No one enjoys paying taxes, but we're reasonable people. I would take more income and a related tax payment any day over no income and no tax obligation. But there is also no reason to be a tax martyr. We can always strive to lower our tax burden, but we should not get so fixated on lowering our taxes that we lower our income instead.

....

Missing the Point

Let me give you an example of the insane tactics some people will try just to pay a smaller tax bill.

*I purchased my first commercial real estate property in 2015 and was trying to rent out an office suite. I had shown the office to only a couple of potential prospects before I had a bite from a man I will call Jesse, a middle-aged man with a full-time job who wanted to open an art studio. But there was an interesting twist to his plan: he only had a couple of students, and he didn't intend to get more. His goal was not to grow a profitable business; he just wanted to grow some **tax write-offs**.*

In fact, he said these exact words as we stood in the parking lot: "I'm making too much money at my job, and I need a tax write-off." He continued, "That's why I need office space instead of doing this at my house. This will give me more deductions."

Of course, as a CPA, I was stunned to hear such ignorance. I had to struggle not to tell him directly what I thought of his idea, which was, "You mean to tell me that you are intentionally trying to spend money that you don't need to spend, in order to pay less in taxes?"

I hope you see the ignorance in Jesse's plan. A deduction is not a direct offset for tax. A deduction is more like a discount. If you don't smoke, but you see a 40 percent discount on cigarettes at your convenience store, would you buy them? I hope not. You had no interest in the cigarettes, and you probably wouldn't even want them if they were free. Why would you purchase them just because they were on sale?

Buying cigarettes you don't want only because they were on sale is equivalent to spending money solely for the purpose of saving on taxes.

A much better way to reduce your taxes is to spend money that the government believes provides so much value that it will offer you lower taxes in return. Use the tax education and savings strategies you find in this book to take more efficient, more productive steps at reducing your tax burden.

TAX TENET #6

Never make tax decisions in a vacuum.

Effective Tax Rate

Instead of focusing on the marginal tax rate, pay more attention to the **effective tax rate,** also called the **average tax rate,** which more accurately reflects the tax rate someone is paying on income. The effective tax rate is simply the total tax paid divided by the total income subject to tax. Many times this is a better way to compare the tax bills of two or more people, especially when you have people who are in the same marginal tax bracket but have different income. They may be in the same marginal tax bracket, but their effective tax rate will be different because they will each pay a different percentage of tax based on their income.

Chapter Summary

✓ *Federal income taxes are progressive. The higher your taxable income, the higher the rate of tax you pay.*

✓ *Your filing status will determine your tax brackets.*

✓ *The marginal tax rate is your highest rate of tax.*

✓ *The effective tax rate is the average tax rate you pay.*

✓ *Tax deductions are more like a discount rather than receiving something for free.*

3

HOW YOU EARN AFFECTS
HOW YOU PAY

After years of intense battles, former U.S. President Donald Trump's tax returns were disclosed to the public at the end of 2022. Reviewing his tax filings from 2015 to 2020 revealed what most expected. Trump paid relatively little in taxes despite his vast empire of real estate. Hard-working individuals with much less wealth than Trump pay more in taxes every year.

I'm not here to talk politics or decide whether this perceived inequity is right or wrong. My point is to show you that not all income is created equal in the eyes of the U.S. government. What type of income you earn will have a significant effect on your tax burden. I've seen many clients who earn over $1 million per year but rarely owe taxes. This isn't because they are cheating or doing anything shady. It's due to the income they earn and how that income is taxed.

When you understand that, you will realize that you have more control over your tax bill than you might realize.

TAX TENET #7
Not all income is created equal.

The income you generate will fit into one of five categories:

- **Earned income**
- **Portfolio income**
- **Rental income**
- **Business income**
- **Capital gains**

Each of these categories has its own rules that must be followed. Understanding the nuances of each category will help you determine which type of income is best to generate if you are judging them from a tax-saving mindset.

The largest differentiators between each category are the tax rate applied, deductions allowed, and whether the amount is subject to the self-employment tax.

Earned Income

This category includes **salaries, wages,** and **self-employment income,** which are taxed the most out of all categories. These items, the most common type of income for most Americans, will be taxed at ordinary tax rates.

SALARIES AND WAGES

Few deductions are available to income earned from salaries and wages, and those deductions are often limited. Wages and salaries are also subject to self-employment tax, which is used to fund the U.S. Social Security and Medicare programs. The self-employment tax is charged on wages, salaries, and self-employment income up to an inflation-adjusted threshold. The Social Security portion is 12.4 percent, and the Medicare portion is 2.9 percent, for a total potential of 15.3 percent. Below the inflation-adjusted threshold, your income is subject to the Social Security and Medicare portions. Above this threshold, only the Medicare portion will apply to your income. Salaries and wages have a benefit over self-employment income because an employee is only responsible for one half of the self-employment taxes, or 7.65 percent. The employer, or the business, will pay the other half.

IN CASE OF AUDIT

Make sure to reference your Form W-2 for how much to report as salaries and wages. This is the form that all employers are required to provide to you each tax year. This form will also record any taxes withheld throughout the year.

IT GOES HERE

Salaries and wages will be reported directly on your Form 1040, individual income tax return.

BEWARE

For 2024, the 15.3 percent Social Security and Medicare tax is applied to income up to $168,600. For earned income above this, only the 2.9 percent Medicare tax applies. This threshold is adjusted for inflation each year. While the Social Security tax drops off at a certain point, there is an additional Medicare tax of 0.9 percent for higher income individuals. Make sure to check the thresholds each year and use TaxStrategiesForEveryone.com as a resource.

SELF-EMPLOYMENT INCOME

Self-employment income is better at reducing your tax burden than salaries and wages are in some ways and worse in others. If you're self-employed, you're generally allowed more deductions than you are as an employee. You can't deduct any of your expenses as an employee. For example, if you drive your car for work, you can't deduct those costs. Instead, you must rely on your employer reimbursing you for those costs. But a self-employed individual can take deductions for the cost of an automobile.

You can also take deductions for the cost of a home office when you're self-employed, but employees cannot. These are only a couple of the deductions you could be entitled to as a self-employed individual that you cannot take as an employee. We'll talk about how to maximize automobile and **home office deductions** in Chapter 8.

IT GOES HERE

Self-employment income can be reported in multiple places, but the most common would be Form 1040, Schedule C.

However, there is also a downside to self-employment income. As a self-employed individual, you are your own employer. This means that you pay all of your self-employment taxes discussed in the previous section. Therefore, you will pay 7.65 percent more in self-employment taxes because there is no employer to pay the other half of the 15.3 percent self-employment tax.

IN CASE OF AUDIT

Activities reported on Schedule C are one of the most audited items on a tax return. If possible, you should figure out a way to report your self-employment income somewhere other than the Schedule C. This will involve the use of legal entities, which are discussed in Chapter 6.

STRATEGY TIP

*Choosing the correct tax entity for your business can reduce the cost of self-employment taxes in certain circumstances. If you operate your business as an **S-corporation**, you must pay yourself a reasonable salary, and only the salary portion of your income will be subject to self-employment tax.*

Portfolio Income

Interest and dividends are considered **portfolio income**. Although there are few deductions allowed against those items, portfolio income does have a significant advantage over **earned income.** That's because portfolio income, while still subject to ordinary tax rates, is not subject to self-employment tax.

TAX TENET #8

Earn income that is immune to self-employment tax. Your wallet will thank you later.

Portfolio income offers extremely limited deductions because investment expenses have not been deductible since tax year 2017. This includes management fees, advisory fees, and costs for financial planners. Investment interest is an exception, but investment interest is an itemized deduction. This makes it less likely you will receive a tax benefit from this deduction.

STRATEGY TIP

If you have a retirement account, like an IRA, make sure to pay any associated fees directly out of the account. They won't be deductible, but this will reduce the taxable income when you withdraw those funds.

IT GOES HERE

Portfolio income is usually reported on Form 1040, Schedule B.

INTEREST INCOME

Interest income includes interest earned from savings accounts, corporate bonds, municipal bonds, treasury bonds, and loans made. Previously, I told you that all income is taxable, unless it's not. One advantage of portfolio income, in addition to avoiding self-employment tax, is that some forms of interest income are not taxable.

Municipal bonds avoid federal income tax although the interest rates earned on municipal bonds are often lower than those earned on other bonds. This is partly because the tax benefits are priced into the rate. However, the relationship between taxable bond interest rates and non-taxable bond interest rates are always in flux, and the interest rates will depend on a variety of factors. The higher your income tax bracket, the greater the benefit of non-taxable municipal bond interest.

STRATEGY TIP

Higher income individuals should consider investing in investments that generate tax-exempt interest.

STRATEGY TIP

Although municipal bonds are non-taxable for federal income tax, they can be taxable for state income tax. Most states will not apply tax to municipal bonds issued by or within them. However, if you invest in a municipal bond from a state where you do not reside, it will be taxable for state purposes. Therefore, it's usually better to invest in municipal bonds issued by your state of residency.

DIVIDEND INCOME

Dividends are distributions of corporate profits to shareholders. These days you would most often receive dividends from publicly traded companies which are taxed as **C-corporations.** Investments in C-corporations, which are often publicly traded, are commonly referred to as stocks. There are not as many private C-corporations in recent years for the reasons you will learn in Chapter 6. However, you can still receive a dividend from a privately held C-corporation; it's just not as common.

Dividends have a unique advantage. Many dividends can be considered **qualified dividends.** If qualified, dividends are taxed at preferential rates, with a maximum tax rate of 20 percent.

I bet you're thinking, "Okay, great, but what is a qualified dividend?" The simple answer is, a qualified dividend is one for which you have held the stock for sixty days before the **ex-dividend date,** which is one market day before the record date. The record date is when a shareholder must be in the corporate books to receive a dividend.

STRATEGY TIP

Investors will pay lower taxes by avoiding self-employment tax and by taking advantage of tax-exempt income and lower tax rates.

BEWARE

Portfolio income can sometimes include capital gains. These would be capital gains from investments, typically stocks. Investments are considered items that are held for appreciation and are not considered a trade or business for tax purposes.

Rental Income

We'll do a deeper dive on rental income and real estate in general in chapters to come. I mention it here to compare to the other types of income. **Rental income** is taxed at ordinary tax brackets; what makes it different from other types of income are the deductions allowed against it.

In addition to being able to deduct essentially any expense necessary to generate rental income, you also receive a **depreciation** deduction, which will be explained in more detail in Chapters 9 and 10. For now, understand that depreciation is a ratable expense taken over a specified number of years for large purchases. Depreciation applies to real estate, excluding land, regardless of whether the value goes up, down, or stays the same. This is one of the largest benefits of owning real estate.

The benefits don't end with depreciation; rental income is also excluded from being subject to self-employment tax.

IT GOES HERE

Rental income is reported on Form 1040, Schedule E.

Business Income

Business income is similar to self-employment income, except that the income flows from a business, not earned directly from your efforts.

IT GOES HERE

Business income is usually reported on Form 1040, Schedule E.

My friend Sarah is a graphic designer and video editor. She does not have any employees. When she takes on a project, she's the one who talks with the clients, bills to the clients, designs the graphics, edits the videos, and delivers the product to the clients. No one else helps her generate that revenue, so Sarah's income is self-employment income.

Business income would be generated from a business, similar to the way Sarah generates her self-employment income. But business income doesn't require you to personally generate every dollar.

There are two frequent examples of business income. The first involves a money—or passive—partner who invested in the business but doesn't actively participate in its day-to-day operations. The other example would be a business owner with employees. Take a busy restaurant with one owner. The owner may be involved in a lot of the day-to-day management of the business, but there are lots of employees necessary to generate the income of the business. There are the servers, the dishwashers, the cooks, and the host. All of these employees are contributing to the income of the business.

The income related to the efforts of the business owner may be earned income (wages or self-employment income), but the income generated by the work of the employees on behalf of the business owner would be business income. If structured correctly, the business income in this case is not subject to self-employment tax.

STRATEGY TIP

Structuring a business correctly up front can save a significant amount of self-employment tax.

Capital Gains and Losses

Simply put, **capital gains** are the result of selling something for more than your **adjusted basis.** Capital gains are special for a couple of reasons:

- Capital gains are subject to lower, preferential rates. In fact, it's possible to have a capital gain taxed at zero percent!
- Capital gains are not subject to self-employment tax.

BEWARE

An item held as inventory in a trade or business is not considered capital gain property. Income from these items will result in ordinary income.

Although I've indicated capital gains are subject to lower tax rates, we need to be mindful of a very important concept: the distinction between long-term capital gains and short-term capital gains. Short-term capital gains come from holding an asset for one year or less before you dispose of it. Long-term capital gains result from holding an asset for more than one year.

I want you to pay a lot of attention to the wording of the last two sentences distinguishing short-term from long-term capital gains. Notice that short-term are those held for one year or less. If you hold an asset for exactly one year, it will still be a short-term capital gain. You must hold an asset for more than one year to qualify as a long-term capital gain. A year and one day is the minimum for long-term capital gains.

You're probably thinking, "Oh jeez, the CPA is getting technical on us here. Who cares?"

You care! Short-term capital gains do not receive the preferential tax treatment so are subject to ordinary income tax rates. Long-term capital gains are taxed at the lower, preferential tax rates. See Table 3.1 for a list of common acronyms associated with capital gains.

Table 3.1. Capital Gains Terms

Legend	
STCG	Short-term capital gain
STCL	Short-term capital loss
LTCG	Long-term capital gain
LTCL	Long-term capital loss

⚠️ BEWARE

Net capital gains from selling collectibles are taxed at a maximum rate of 28 percent. Collectibles include coins, art, stamps, antiques, metals, gems, and any alcoholic beverages.

So far we've addressed capital gains, but what about capital losses? A net capital loss results when you combine your short-term capital gains with your short-term capital losses and then net your long-term capital gains with your long-term capital losses. You would then net your short-term gain or loss with your long-term gain or loss. If the combination of your short-term gains and your long-term gains is negative, it means you have a net capital loss.

Individuals with a net capital loss can offset a maximum of $3,000 of their other income. Other income includes all the items discussed in the previous categories. The $3,000 limit applies whether you're filing Single or Married Filing Jointly. However, if Married Filing Separate then each spouse is limited to $1,500. In the event that your capital loss is greater than this limit, you can carry forward the excess amount indefinitely. The carryforward amount can be used to offset capital gain income in the future. The carryforward will be included in determining whether there is a net capital gain or net capital loss. As long as there is a net capital loss in any given tax year, the $3,000 and $1,500 limits will apply. See Table 3.2 for an example of a net capital loss and how it's limited and Table 3.3 for an example of a net capital gain and which tax rates apply.

Table 3.2. Net capital loss subject to limitation

Step 1: Net STCG and STCL	STCG	$10,000
	STCL	($4,000)
	Net STCG(L)	$6,000
Step 2: Net LTCG and LTCL	LTCG	$5,000
	LTCL	($20,000)
	Net LTCG(L)	($15,000)
Step 3: Net STCG(L) with LTCG(L)	Net STCG(L)	$6,000
	Net LTCG(L)	($15,000)
	Net capital gain (loss)*	($9,000)

*The loss is limited to $3,000 or $1,500 each year.

Table 3.3. Tax rates for net capital gain

Step 1: Net STCG and STCL	STCG	$10,000
	STCL	($4,000)
	Net STCG(L)	$6,000
Step 2: Net LTCG and LTCL	LTCG	$5,000
	LTCL	$2,000
	Net LTCG(L)	$7,000
Step 3: Net STCG(L) with LTCG(L)	Net STCG(L)	$6,000
	Net LTCG(L)	$7,000
	Net capital gain (loss)*	$13,000

* The net short-term capital gain will be taxed at ordinary income tax rates and the net long-term capital gain will be taxed at preferential capital gain rates.

TAX TENET #9

Capital gains are great, but capital losses are unbearable.

....

C-corporations Don't Play Well with Capital Gains or Losses

The corporate rules for capital gains and losses are similar in terms of the netting process. However, the rules for C-corporations differ in two important ways. First, a net capital gain, whether short-term or long-term, will be taxed at the ordinary income rates for a C-corporation. There is no preferential lower tax rate for C-corporations.

Further, a net capital loss cannot be deducted at all. A net capital loss can be carried back three years and/or forward five years, only to offset other capital gain income. If not utilized in any of these years, it is lost. This is one of the many reasons businesses don't use C-corporations anymore.

....

IT GOES HERE

Capital gains and losses are reported on Form 1040, Schedule D.

It should be clear by now that the type of income you have can dramatically affect the amount of tax you pay. I've included Table 3.4 to help you quickly compare the various types of income and how they are taxed.

Table 3.4. Comparing characteristics of income categories

	Earned Income	Portfolio Income	Rental Income	Business Income	Capital Gains
Preferential tax rates	No	Qualified dividends and tax-exempt interest	No	No	Long-term capital gains only
Self-employment tax	Yes	No	No	No	No
Deductions allowed	Few for salaries and wages but many for self-employed income	Interest expense	Many	Many	You can elect interest expense

....

Chapter Summary

✓ *Wages and salaries have the fewest opportunities for deductions.*

✓ *Self-employment tax planning can greatly reduce your tax burden.*

✓ *Two major differences between the five different types of income are the tax rate and the availability of deductions against the income.*

✓ *Hold capital gain property for more than a year before selling to receive preferential rates.*

✓ *See Table 3.4 for a comparison of tax features of the five types of income.*

4

PASSIVE INCOME: TAX FRIEND OR FOE

If you've been anywhere near the investment world, you have probably heard of the term **passive income.** To earn passive income you don't have to trade hours for money. That sounds pretty good, right?

Well, passive income is not always so great when you're looking to minimize your taxes. You actually want the opposite of passive income many times.

Notice I said "many times" and not "all the time." This is one of those "it depends" situations that we talked about previously. You'll notice you generally want to avoid passive status when an activity will generate a tax loss, but your only other income is from non-passive sources. If you only have passive income (not losses), then the other reason you may want to avoid the passive status is to lower your tax rate. We'll talk about this at the end of the chapter.

To better understand situations when you may want passive activities and when you may not, we need to talk about what a passive activity is. The good news is the IRS definition of passive income is different from what the traditional investor's definition may be, and you can put that to work in your favor.

Material Participation

Passive income—or loss—is any income (loss) from an activity in which you do not materially participate. A taxpayer will be considered to have materially participated in an activity if they meet any of the following requirements:

1. The taxpayer's participation is for more than 500 hours.

2. The taxpayer's participation constitutes substantially all of the participation in the activity by all individuals (including nonowners) for the tax year.

3. The taxpayer participates in the activity for more than 100 hours during the tax year, and such participation is not less than the participation of any other person.

4. The taxpayer's activity is a significant participation activity for the tax year, and aggregate participation in all significant participation activities during the year exceeds 500 hours. A significant participation activity is one in which the taxpayer has more than 100 hours of participation during the tax year but fails to satisfy any other test for material participation.

5. The taxpayer has materially participated in the activity for any five of the ten tax years immediately proceeding the tax year in question. The five tax years need not be consecutive.

6. The taxpayer has materially participated in any three preceding years if the activity is a defined personal service activity. A personal service activity is one that involves the performance of personal services in the fields of health, law, engineering, architecture, accounting, actuarial science, performing arts, consulting, or any other trade or business in which capital is not a material income-producing factor.

7. The taxpayer participates regularly, continuously, and substantially, taking into account all facts and circumstances.

These are the seven factors that the IRS will look at to determine whether you materially participate in an activity. If you meet any of the first six factors, you will be deemed to materially participate. You'll notice the last factor, seven, is somewhat vague. This is a catch-all for situations where a taxpayer is not meeting one of the first six factors but should really still be deemed as materially participating. Let's look at a couple common examples.

NO MATERIAL PARTICIPATION EXAMPLE #1

Don is a full-time software engineer. His friend Justin approaches him about a new beverage company he is planning to open. Justin is very confident the company will be profitable after a three-year start-up period, and he wants Don to invest in the business. Justin provides the business plan, projections, and legal documents for Don to review. After careful consideration, Don decides this is a good investment and gives Justin's business $100,000. Don does have some voting rights in the business for major transactions, but otherwise is not involved in the daily management of the company. Justin and his team are continuously involved in the business. Don's main contribution to the company is the capital.

Clearly, with no daily involvement and simply reviewing financial statements and taking a couple of votes throughout the year, Don isn't going to spend enough time on this activity to meet any of the first six IRS guidelines for material participation. Don also won't meet the catch-all because his involvement is not regular and continuous. Don's investment in the beverage business would be considered a passive activity.

NO MATERIAL PARTICIPATION EXAMPLE #2

After investing in Justin's company, Don is approached by another friend, Kyle, who wants to develop a new app. Kyle already has the programmers and capital he needs to get the app off the ground. However, Kyle knows Don has a lot of knowledge in this area and connections that could be useful for his new company.

So Kyle offers Don a 10 percent profit interest in the new business if Don will consult with the other owners about the direction of the app and provide resources to the company. Don agrees. Throughout the first couple of years, Don spends about 120 hours per year making a few introductions for the company and providing direction to its programmers.

Although Don did spend more than 100 hours specified in IRS guideline 3, he was not participating for more hours than anyone else. Don also clearly doesn't meet the 500-hour factor, and as far as the catch-all seventh factor, Don often went for months without doing any consulting work or making introductions for the company. His activity was very sporadic, and based on the company's needs—not regular and continuous. Although Don provided time and knowledge to Kyle's company, rather than just offering up capital as he did to Justin, his involvement does not rise to the level of material participation. This activity would also be considered passive for Don.

MATERIAL PARTICIPATION EXAMPLE #1

Our friend Don decides he could put his expertise to good use and make a little profit by selling cloud storage services to other businesses. He spends his weekends working on the business and a lot of mornings making sales calls. It's not important for Don to add up the number of hours he spends on the cloud-storage business because he does not get help from others. So, based on IRS guideline 2, his work "constitutes substantially all of the participation in the activity." Therefore, Don will be treated as materially participating in the activity.

MATERIAL PARTICIPATION EXAMPLE #2

After a couple of years working the phones trying to interest business owners in cloud storage services, Don recognizes he has technical expertise but isn't the best salesperson. So he decides to reach out to his buddy Erin, who is a great salesperson. They agree to be 50/50 partners with Don running the back end of the business and Erin making the sales. Don spends at least 500 hours on his part of the business during the year, so he meets the first factor in determining material participation even though Erin is also participating in the activity.

While Don likely also met the seventh factor for material participation, it's better if he can meet one of the other six. The last factor is very much based on the facts and circumstances and therefore can be subject to interpretation. It's much better to meet at least one of the "bright line" tests for material participation so there aren't as many questions as to how you characterize your activities on your tax returns. It will also be much easier to document hours spent on an activity, which is key to the first six factors.

IN CASE OF AUDIT

Try not to rely on the seventh factor for material participation as it will be the hardest to prove.

Hopefully you now have a better understanding of what is considered a passive or nonpassive activity. Next, let's discuss why it matters and what actions you can take to create the best tax outcome.

Passive Losses Only Offset Passive Income

Passive income sounds pretty good, so why wouldn't I want passive income when it comes to my taxes? For starters, passive losses can only offset passive income. In other words, the income from your salary cannot be reduced by passive losses. Your salary is active or earned income, not passive. This has tripped up more than a few people.

There are absolutely great tax benefits to passive investments, but you have to know the rules so you can take advantage of the benefits. I have seen some poor outcomes when people only partially understand the passive income rules.

I had a client who wanted to start investing in real estate, passively, after they had heard about all the great tax benefits. Without talking to me, this client invested in a real estate deal with a large developer, and the investment showed a loss of about $50,000 in the first year, which is common. There are generally tax losses the first year a project is completed as the investment is still in the process of being stabilized.

My client was excited when he handed me his tax documents that year, expecting he would be receiving a large refund because of the investment losses. But my heart sank as I learned he was only a limited investor in the project; he was not involved in any of the management or decision-making and had spent no time on the activity. His only involvement was reading the agreements and wiring funds to the developer.

I quickly realized my client was not going to receive the outcome he desired on this investment, at least not that year, because his only income was active income from his business and the salary that he drew from it. He needed passive income to take advantage of the investment losses. See Figure 4.1 for an illustration regarding passive income.

BEWARE

Do not confuse passive income with the portfolio income we discussed in the previous chapter. Portfolio income—such as interest and dividends—is not considered passive income. Since these items are in a completely different tax bucket, they will not help you deduct any passive losses you may have.

Figure 4.1. It's not always easy to determine what is passive income.

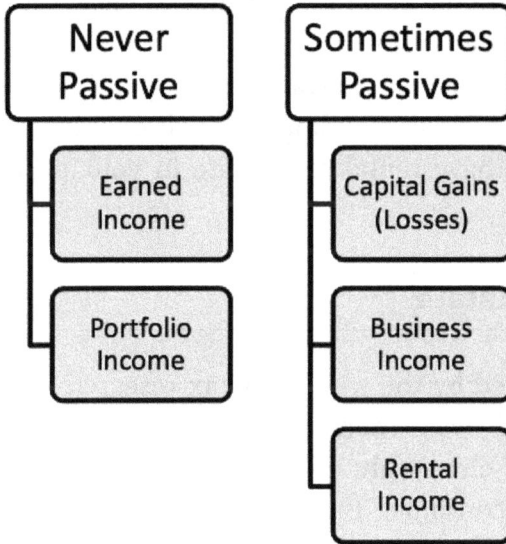

```
┌─────────────┐   ┌─────────────┐
│    Never    │   │  Sometimes  │
│   Passive   │   │   Passive   │
└─────────────┘   └─────────────┘
    │                 │
    │  ┌──────────┐    │  ┌──────────────┐
    ├──│  Earned  │    ├──│ Capital Gains│
    │  │  Income  │    │  │   (Losses)   │
    │  └──────────┘    │  └──────────────┘
    │  ┌──────────┐    │  ┌──────────────┐
    └──│Portfolio │    ├──│   Business   │
       │  Income  │    │  │    Income    │
       └──────────┘    │  └──────────────┘
                       │  ┌──────────────┐
                       └──│    Rental    │
                          │    Income    │
                          └──────────────┘
```

If you only have nonpassive income, or active income, then losses from a new activity that is passive will not help you. There are two ways to solve this problem and take advantage of losses.

The first option is to try converting a passive activity into an active activity. You can use the seven factors for material participation above to determine which one would be the easiest to meet in your specific case. Many times, however, this may not be practical.

In this case, a good approach is to find another passive activity that will generate income. This allows you to earn income from one passive activity that is sheltered by tax from the one generating losses.

In our first example above, Don did not materially participate, but if he expects losses from this investment for a few years, he would do well to find another passive investment that will generate income. Perhaps Don decides to invest in an apartment building with his friend Ken. Don won't participate in the business and will only provide capital. Ken negotiated a great deal on the apartment and expects to generate income immediately. Don will be able to use his losses from the beverage business to offset the income from the apartment investment.

Speaking of rental real estate, the IRS has special treatment for this category. Understanding this will be critical for your tax planning if you have rental real estate in your portfolio, so let's tackle that next.

Rental Real Estate

I'm often haunted by the words my tax research professor would repeat over and over when I was working toward my master's degree. "There's almost always an exception," she would say. And then she would continue, "But it doesn't stop there. There's usually an exception to the exception."

Sometimes the exceptions run many layers deep. Rental real estate offers one of those exceptions to the general rule because it is passive by default regardless of whether you meet the material participation requirements.

While rental real estate is the exception to material participation, there is an exception to this exception. Well, actually, there are two exceptions to this exception. They come in the form of active rental real estate participation and the materially participating real estate professional. Both of these exceptions function to convert what would be passive rental real estate income by default to nonpassive. In other words, by default you can only offset rental real estate losses with passive income. But through these two exceptions, you have the opportunity to offset rental real estate losses with your active income.

If you do not have losses from any of your activities, then it may not be as critical to convert activities from passive to nonpassive or add a passive activity that will generate income to absorb those losses. The goal of converting passive activities to nonpassive activities is generally to absorb losses against other income. With that said, there is one other reason to convert passive activities to nonpassive, even if there is income, which will be discussed toward the end of this chapter.

ACTIVE RENTAL REAL ESTATE SPECIAL ALLOWANCE

Qualifying your rental real estate for the active rental real estate special allowance is actually quite easy most of the time, but there are strict limits on your ability to use active rental real estate losses to offset your other income. There are two limitations for taking advantage of these tax losses, as illustrated in Figure 4.2.

Figure 4.2. There are limitations to active rental real estate losses.

Limitation #1	• Limited to $25,000 of active rental real estate losses. • Unused losses will carry over to future years.
Limitation #2	• The $25,000 limit is reduced when your AGI exceeds $100,000. • Limited 50 percent for every dollar over $100,000. • No deduction when your AGI reaches $150,000.

BEWARE

This exception only applies to rental real estate, not to rental of equipment or airplanes. It may also not apply to certain short-term rentals, or hotels or nursing homes depending on the rate of customer turnover and the level of services provided.

Limiting the Exception

Josh has an active rental real estate loss of $25,000. His AGI is $110,000, and he is a Single tax filer. Therefore, his limitation is reduced by 50 percent of $10,000, the amount of his AGI that exceeds $100,000.

Therefore, he can deduct only $20,000 of his $25,000 rental real estate losses for the current year. The remaining $5,000 will carry forward to future years.

Both the $25,000 maximum and the $100,000 AGI phaseout apply to Single filers and Married Filing Jointly filers. These limitations are cut in half for those Married Filing Separately.

Okay, great, so we know how the special allowance for active rental real estate works, but what actually qualifies? There are three main criteria for this special allowance:

- **You must own at least 10 percent of the rental.**
- **You cannot be a *limited partner.***
- **You must actively participate.**

The first two requirements are fairly self-explanatory, so let's focus on the last one. Although not specifically defined, it's clear that the threshold for active participation is meant to be less strict than that of material participation. To actively participate, you must be involved in the making of management decisions or at least arranging for others to provide the services. For example, you would be actively participating if you approve new tenants, decide on rental terms, approve large repairs, or make other similar decisions. Unlike material participation, you do not need to meet hour requirements.

> ⚠️ **BEWARE**
>
> *Rental properties that are operated under a net lease, for example a triple net lease, will not likely meet active participation requirements. A triple net lease makes the tenant responsible for the real estate taxes, insurance, and scheduling repairs. In this arrangement, the property owner is not involved in enough management decisions to meet the criteria.*

The active participation rules are designed for those who are not full-time real estate professionals, which makes it a great exception for those who have other full-time or part-time jobs or businesses.

When I was starting my career as a CPA, I knew investing in real estate would be critical to my financial independence. Because I was putting in about 2,400 hours a year as a CPA, I would manage my rental properties on weekends and after my regular workdays, so there was no way I would be able to meet the material participation threshold or reach real estate professional status. I could, however, easily meet the active participation requirements, which allowed me to offset some of my earnings as a CPA with rental real estate losses.

I should make it clear that qualifying for this special allowance does not mean the rental activities are not still passive. This exception only means that you can use the allowed losses to offset other income. The activities will still be passive. We'll go over how to avoid passive characterization for rental real estate next.

MATERIALLY PARTICIPATING REAL ESTATE PROFESSIONAL

Real estate professional status is the holy grail of tax qualifications when it comes to investing in real estate. Qualifying for this status allows you to offset rental real estate losses against any type of income. However, let me be clear. The materially participating real estate professional status only removes the default passive treatment of rental real estate for taxpayers. After qualifying for this status, the taxpayer must still materially participate in each of the rental real estate activities. Similar to active rental real estate discussed previously qualifying as a materially participating real estate professional and materially participating in the rental estate activities, will have the effect of removing the passive status from those activities.

A taxpayer will qualify for real estate professional status when they meet both of the following:

- Spend more than half of their personal service hours in real property trades or businesses; and

- Spend more than 750 hours in real property trades or businesses.

IN CASE OF AUDIT

You should keep a log of what activities you perform each week on real property trades or businesses, especially if it isn't obvious that you meet the hours requirements. Whenever you have earned income from a source other than real estate, the IRS is prone to question your status as a real estate professional. Don't become one of the many court cases denying this status to a taxpayer.

The first requirement speaks to how much of your working hours are spent in real property trades or business compared to other trades or businesses—as an owner or any employee. For example, a software engineer job would not be considered a real property **trade or business.** So, if you are a software engineer *and* a real estate professional, you would need to spend more hours in a real property trade or business than hours as a software engineer in order to qualify for materially participating real estate professional status.

Practically speaking, it's difficult—if not impossible—for someone with a full-time job or business in a field that is not real estate to qualify for this status. A full-time job would typically be considered 2,080 hours per year. This would mean you would have to work 2,081 hours in a real property trade or business—in addition to what you work at your other job—to qualify. People who have rental real estate as an investment and also work a full-time job will almost never qualify for this designation.

However, it's a different story if your full-time job is already a real property trade or business. So, what the heck is a real property trade or business? Here's your list:

- **Real property development**
- **Real property redevelopment**
- **Construction**
- **Reconstruction**
- **Acquisition**
- **Conversion**
- **Rental**
- **Operation**
- **Management**
- **Leasing**
- **Brokerage**

BEWARE

Real property appraisers and real property lenders are not considered to be in a real property trade or business.

STRATEGY TIP

If married, only one spouse needs to meet the materially participating real estate professional requirement for both spouses to receive the benefits.

Your job is not done as soon as you acquire status as a real estate professional. You didn't think the IRS would make it that easy, did you? The next step is meeting the material participation tests described earlier for each of your rental trades or businesses. The more rental properties you own, the more difficult this will be. It will also be difficult to retain status if you co-own rentals with someone else who may be more involved than you are. This could prevent you from meeting the material participation requirements on properties that you co-own.

Think of someone who owns multiple apartment complexes or a large portfolio of rental properties. They probably aren't meeting the 500-hour requirement for each property. Someone who owns five rental properties would already be spending 2,500 hours a year between all of them (500 each), assuming they didn't meet one of the other six out of seven ways to prove material participation.

STRATEGY TIP

Luckily, the IRS allows you to consider all your rental activities together in determining material participation as long as you elect to do so. Therefore, if you have five rental properties and you spend 100 hours in each, you would have 500 total hours, which would allow you to meet the first option for material participation without having to materially participate in each rental activity. Work with your tax advisor to determine whether this solution will work for you.

SHORT-TERM RENTALS

These days a discussion on passive activity rules wouldn't be complete without addressing short-term rentals. The passive activity rules were passed with the Tax Reform Act of 1986, well before the advent of Airbnb, VRBO, or other short-term rental services.

You may assume that because these activities involve real estate rentals, the rules for active participation and materially participating real estate professional status would apply. You would be wrong.

The trick with interpreting the internal revenue code is to pay attention to how the IRS defines terms. Their definitions do not always match up with our definitions because the law is usually quite specific—especially when it comes to exceptions. The exceptions are meant to fit only a specific set of circumstances.

So, you need to be very aware that the following are exempted from the definition of "rental activity" for passive loss rules:

- **Those for which the average period of customer use is seven days or less; and**

- **Those for which the average period of customer use is thirty days or less, and "significant personal services" are provided.**

The large majority of short-term rentals will average a nightly stay of seven or less, therefore escaping classification as a rental activity. While the active participation and materially participating real estate professional exceptions would no longer apply, there's a silver lining to this classification: the short-term rental is not considered a rental activity according to the IRS so it is not a per se passive activity. Thus, most short-term rentals can avoid passive loss rules simply by meeting the material participation requirements described at the beginning of the chapter rather than the more stringent standards established for rental real estate activities. You do not need to be a materially participating real estate professional to deduct losses from your short-term rental activities against your other income.

Net Investment Income Tax

We've focused the previous sections of this chapter on how to utilize tax losses and some ways to convert otherwise passive activities into active activities. However, remember I mentioned at the beginning there is also a consideration when you have passive income. The net investment income tax is an additional 3.8 percent tax that is levied on certain income once you rise above the threshold income levels. This tax generally applies to individuals, but trusts and estates can also be subject to this tax, which generally applies to income from interest, dividends, annuities, royalties, capital gains, rents, and passive business income.

This tax will not be levied on income derived in the ordinary course of a trade or business that is not considered passive. It is fairly difficult to avoid this tax on investment income for interest, dividends, annuities, and royalties because these are rarely considered trade or business income since they are typically in the portfolio income bucket.

Rents and business income are a different story. You can use the strategies discussed previously to either avoid passive characterization or acquire another activity or activities that will generate passive losses to offset the income from your passive rents and passive business income. For rental income, this will force you to navigate the materially participating real estate professional and short-term rental rules even if you have income from these activities.

BEWARE

Since the active rental real estate special allowance does not prevent a rental activity from being passive, qualifying for this allowance will not avoid the net investment income tax. You will need to materially participate in the case of a short-term rental and you will need to both be a materially participating real estate professional and materially participate in the rental activities for other rental activities in order to avoid this tax.

You will only be subject to the net investment income tax if your income is above the thresholds detailed in Table 4.1. These thresholds are not adjusted for inflation each year.

Table 4.1. Net investment income tax

Filing Status	Threshold
Single, Head of Household	$200,000
Married Filing Jointly; Surviving Spouse	$250,000
Married Filing Separately	$125,000

....

Net Investment Income Tax Example

Let's assume a taxpayer filing Single status has $190,000 of wages and $20,000 of investment income. The total income for this taxpayer therefore is $210,000. The threshold level is $200,000 for a Single filer. This means only the income above $200,000, which is also investment income, will be subject to the 3.8 percent tax. Only $10,000 out of the total $20,000 of investment income exceeds this threshold, meaning that is what will be subject to the net investment income tax.

Let's change the example. The wages of the individual are now $205,000, and the investment income is $20,000, which means the total income is $225,000, with $25,000 exceeding the threshold. However, only $20,000 of that is considered investment income. Therefore, only the $20,000 of investment income will be subject to the net investment income tax. The $5,000 of wages that is over the $200,000 threshold is not subject to that tax.

....

Chapter Summary

✓ *We are most often concerned about the ability to take tax losses when we are dealing with passive activities.*

✓ *You cannot deduct your passive income against earned income or portfolio income.*

✓ *If you have a passive activity that is generating a loss, you want to either convert it to nonpassive or add a passive activity that generates income to offset the passive loss.*

✓ *Rental real estate is passive by default, but you can qualify for either active participation or materially participating real estate professional to benefit from rental real estate losses*

✓ *Short-term rental real estate provides a loophole to the default passive classification of rental real estate.*

✓ *You may want to avoid having passive activities even if they generate income in order to avoid the net investment income tax.*

5

GETTING THE CREDITS
YOU DESERVE

Tax credits. These are the crème de la crème of tax benefits. Do not confuse tax credits with tax deductions. There is an important distinction.

A tax credit is a direct offset against your tax burden, which can fully cover the cost of your outflow in some instances. If you have a tax credit of $1,000, then your tax bill will be reduced by that same amount.

Deductions, on the other hand, are more like discounts for your expenses. A deduction lowers your taxable income, which indirectly reduces your tax burden, but it will not fully offset the cost you incurred to create the deduction. A $1,000 deduction for someone in the 24 percent marginal tax bracket will receive a benefit akin to a 24 percent discount. Your net cost after the discount (deduction) is $760 ($1,000 less $240 in tax savings). This is certainly a nice benefit, but often times doesn't compare to the ability to take a tax credit. For an example of this using a single taxpayer and the tax brackets, see Table 5.1.

Table 5.1. Tax deduction vs. tax credit

	With Tax Deduction	With Tax Credit
Gross income	$110,000	$110,000
Tax deduction	($1,000)	$0
Taxable income	$109,000	$110,000
Tax (before credits)	$19,203	$19,443
Tax credit	$0	($1,000)
Tax due	$19,203	$18,443

Tax credits provide great insight into the goals of the government —and special interest groups. The government offers tax credits for what brings the most important value to society, in the opinion of the federal government. You will often see which direction the government would like to steer society by examining what it is willing to give taxpayers credits for.

For example, consider the energy incentives passed in 2022 as part of the Inflation Reduction Act (IRA). That act demonstrated that the federal government believes the country needs to make major shifts toward alternative energy and energy-saving actions. Tax credits for energy incentives existed before this law passed, but most of those credits were greatly improved and new ones were added through the IRA.

Recognize this: when tax credits are available, the government wants you to take action. Remember the idea that when you create value, you can lower your taxes? That concept is plainly seen by how the government creates and uses tax credits. If you can create or implement a change that will allow you to qualify for a tax credit, you have created value in the government's eyes and you deserve a lower tax bill.

Usually it's pretty easy to see what the government sees as important. Therefore, if you know that you will be spending money on something that could align with an area the government values highly, check to see if there are any tax credits available for what good or service you are about to create or an action you are about to take.

TAX TENET #10

Follow the credits.

Is It Refundable?

It's important to understand whether a tax credit is considered refundable or not. Refundable means you can actually offset your tax liability completely and any remaining credit will result in cash back.

For example, with a refundable tax credit, if you had a $600 tax liability and a $1,000 credit, then the credit would first reduce your tax liability to $0 and the remaining $400 left would be refunded to you.

If the credit is not refundable, check to see whether it can carry over for use to offset your tax liability in future years. You will also need to know how long the credit would carry over. Some credits are lost if they are not used in the year you earn them, but many credits will be eligible to carry over.

In the next few pages, I describe some tax credits that are available to businesses and others that are available to individual taxpayers. There is some overlap in terms of similar credits and items covered. However, there is generally a greater benefit to credits you can take advantage of in a business.

A lot of the individual tax credits will be phased out at certain income levels, meaning higher income individuals will not benefit from them, at least not as much. For businesses, the credits are rarely phased out based on income, allowing low-earning and high-earning businesses to benefit. This is another example of how the government often values and favors business initiatives over individual initiatives.

Despite the greater value on business credits, you'll see there is still great value to individual tax credits, and you certainly do not want to ignore these opportunities. Let's examine some specific credits that can benefit you.

Individual Tax Credits

EDUCATION CREDITS

Encouraging education has been a longtime favorite activity for the federal government because higher levels of education are highly valued in the government's eyes. Guess what this means? That's right; this area is ripe with credits available for those ready to take advantage.

Two types of education credits are available: the lifetime learning credit (LLC) and the American opportunity tax credit (AOTC). (The LLC or the Lifetime Learning Credit is not to be confused with the limited liability company that we will discuss in Chapter 6.) Both of these credits require the following:

1. **Must be used for qualified education expenses.**

2. **The student must be enrolled at an *eligible education institution.***

3. **You, your spouse, or a dependent that you claim on your tax return is the student.**

Qualified education expenses are tuition, fees, and other related expenses for enrollment. The AOTC also allows you to include expenses for books, supplies, and equipment needed for a student's course of study.

There are also expenses that could be paid as a result of enrolling and attending school that would not qualify for the credits. These expenses are:

- **Room and board**

- **Insurance**

- **Medical expenses**

- **Transportation**

- **Similar personal, living, or family expenses.**

American opportunity tax credit. The AOTC is typically the most beneficial education tax credit and can be maximized for a credit of $2,500. This is nothing to sneeze at.

IN CASE OF AUDIT

If you are claiming the AOTC, make sure to check that the education institution checked the correct boxes on the Form 1098-T they issue at the end of the year. This form indicates the amount of tuition paid and whether it was for a graduate degree or not. You can't take the AOTC for a graduate degree so make sure that box isn't accidently checked it if doesn't apply to you. The 1098-T is sent to the IRS and will be matched with what you report on your tax return.

The AOTC is based on 100 percent of the first $2,000 of qualifying expenses and 25 percent of the next $2,000 of qualifying expenses. So you will maximize the credit after you have incurred at least $4,000 of qualified education expenses. Additionally, up to 40 percent of the AOTC can be refundable, meaning up to $1,000. If you have a tax liability of $1,500 before the credit, $1,500 will bring your tax liability to zero and the remaining $1,000 will be refunded to you when filing your tax return.

⚠️ **BEWARE**

The AOTC can only be claimed for the first four years of higher education. You can't claim this credit for graduate degrees.

Note that many credits and deductions, particularly for individual taxpayers, will phase out at certain income levels. This is another example of the progressive nature of the U.S. tax system, and it means that lower-income and lower-middle-income taxpayers tend to benefit the most from tax credits. Table 5.2 shows the income phaseout levels for the AOTC. These are not adjusted for inflation each year.

Table 5.2. AOTC income phaseout levels

	Single Filers	**Married Filing Jointly**
Full credit	Up to $80,000 AGI	Up to $160,000 AGI
Partial credit	AGI between $80,000–$90,000	AGI between $160,000–$180,000
No credit	AGI above $90,000	AGI above $180,000

You're on Your Own, Kid

I had a client who was a Boeing executive bringing in good money. His son was attending college—which wasn't cheap. I don't know if you've heard the news in the last twenty years, but colleges aren't getting any cheaper.

My client qualified for the AOTC, but his income level meant he would not be able to receive any of the benefit for the credit. He was completely phased out of it. I asked a few questions and discovered the son could actually claim himself, rather than allowing my client to claim him as a dependent on his tax return. My client was not receiving any benefit for claiming his son that year, so the change wouldn't hurt him.

His son was working a part-time job, possibly as a Starbucks barista. With his full-time schooling and part-time work, you can imagine that my client's son had far less income than my client did. I told them that if the son claimed himself, he could take the AOTC on his tax return—even though my client had actually paid for the tuition expenses.

The son was able to receive the AOTC credit that year, helping slightly with the burden of increasing education costs. This is a great strategy for higher income earners who would not benefit from the credit themselves.

....

Lifetime learning credit (LLC). The LLC garners a lower tax benefit at a maximum of $2,000 but makes up for the lower benefit with its less restrictive nature. Unlike the AOTC, the LLC can be claimed for an unlimited number of years of higher education, which is great for those going back to school or continuing on past four years of higher education into graduate programs.

Nor does the LLC require that you be pursuing a degree, which makes it a good option for business owners or employees simply trying to expand their knowledge. You can claim this credit for courses to acquire or improve job skills, and no formal educational credential is required.

The LLC has the same income phaseouts as the AOTC, which are shown in Table 5.2. However, the LLC is not refundable at all. You will want to make sure anyone who claims this credit will actually have a tax liability to offset with the credit.

STRATEGY TIP

While you can claim both the AOTC and LLC on the same tax return, you cannot claim them both for the same student or for the same qualifying expenses.

SAVER'S CREDIT

You must have heard about the Social Security and retirement crises at least once in the last couple of decades. Well, this is a credit to incentivize people to save for retirement. This credit can be for 50 percent, 20 percent, or 10 percent of the contributions that you make to **Individual Retirement Accounts (IRAs)** or employer-sponsored retirement plans.

This can be a helpful credit, but the income limitations are very low for claiming this. For 2024, there's no credit for single filers making more than $38,250 or married taxpayers filing jointly making more than $76,500. These amounts are adjusted for inflation, so make sure to check for updates and reference TaxStrategiesForEveryone.com.

EARNED INCOME TAX CREDIT

Our tax system is so progressive that the lowest income taxpayers often don't incur any tax liability due to various tax credits in conjunction with their lower tax rates. The earned income tax credit is intended to assist low-income to "moderate"-income taxpayers. I put moderate in quotation marks because I doubt most would consider this credit as a benefit for middle-income taxpayers.

The credit is based on your income level, filing status, and number of qualifying children. In addition, if you have too much investment income, you will not be eligible. The majority of the income must be earned income.

I'm not going to offer up many details on this credit because of the income requirements. I don't think this is a credit you should focus on. It's not worth sacrificing income in order to get credits or lower your tax liability.

CHILD AND DEPENDENT CARE CREDIT

The government recognizes and rewards those who work because it contributes to the economy, and this credit assists families by effectively lowering the cost of child and dependent care to help keep people in the workforce. The credit is based on the amount of work-related expenses and number of qualifying persons. A qualifying person is generally a child you claim as a dependent who was under the age of thirteen when care was provided. However, it can also include a spouse or individual who is incapable of self-care and lived with you for more than half the year.

Work-related expenses are the costs paid for child or dependent care that allowed you or your spouse to work. You can consider up to $3,000 of work-related expenses if you have one qualifying person and up to $6,000 of work-related expenses if you have two or more qualifying persons. For 2024, you would figure your credit by multiplying the eligible work-related expenses by 35 percent if your income is $15,000 or less. This percentage reduces until it reaches 20 percent once your income is over $43,000. These amounts are not adjusted for inflation each year.

Higher income families receive lower levels of credit, and the rising cost of childcare may make this credit less attractive. Noticing the trend yet? Higher income individuals and families receive fewer tax credits. So higher income individuals should focus more on generating income from sources other than earned income to receive the best tax benefits.

ENERGY EFFICIENT HOME IMPROVEMENT CREDIT

Up to a 30 percent credit is offered for the cost of eligible home improvement costs. The improvements will need to meet the government's designated energy-efficient standards, which should be noted by the product manufacturer. Figure 5.1 shows which products can be eligible for the credit.

Figure 5.1. Multiple energy-efficient products can be eligible for a tax credit.

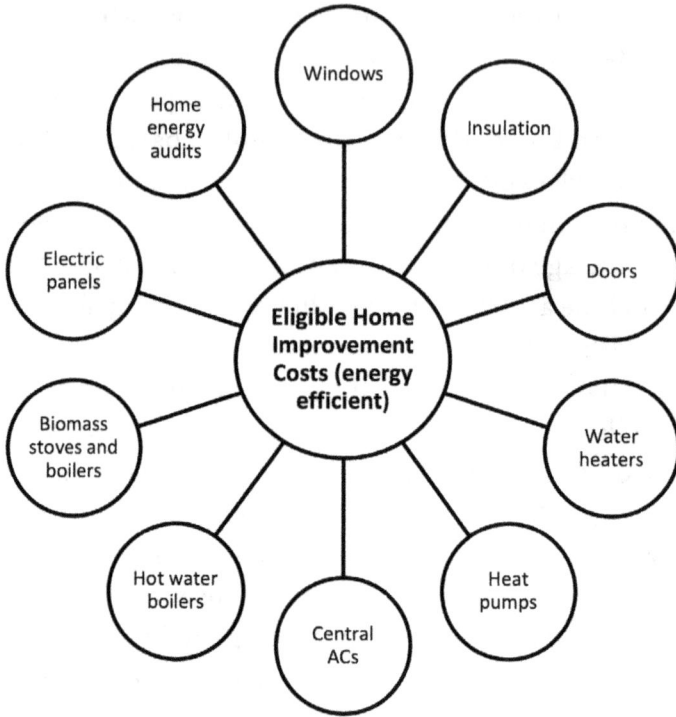

There is a $1,200 annual limit on the credit each year. Translation: you can receive a credit for up to $4,000 of energy-efficient home improvements because the credit is for 30 percent of the total spent.

Some improvements will allow for a larger credit, up to $2,000 each year. Make sure you check which credits are available before you make improvements. It's always nice to have someone else help foot the bill for improving your home's energy efficiency.

STRATEGY TIP

Spread your energy-efficient home improvements out to maximize the credit each year. If you spend more than $4,000 a year on improvements, you won't receive a credit for the additional amounts.

RESIDENTIAL CLEAN ENERGY CREDIT

You're entitled to a 30 percent credit on the amounts spent for installing qualifying systems that use solar, wind, geothermal, or fuel cell power to produce electricity, heat water, or control the temperature of your home.

There is no annual or lifetime dollar limit for this credit, except for fuel cell property.

> **BEWARE**
>
> *Both the energy-efficient home improvement credit and residential clean energy credit can be claimed only on your main home. You cannot claim these credits for a rental property.*

Business Tax Credits

RETIREMENT PLAN CREDITS

The U.S. retirement and Social Security dilemma has been a growing issue that needs solving. The government stepped up their game on incentivizing businesses to provide retirement plans for their employees with the Secure Act 2.0 passed in 2022.

As part of that act, the federal government will fully subsidize the costs of setting up a retirement plan for certain businesses, and it offers tax credits for employers who make contributions to retirement plans on behalf of employees.

Businesses that offer retirement plans can be more competitive in attracting and retaining talent, and they can gain an even greater edge by giving retirement benefits. Add in the federal tax advantages and everyone wins! Employers benefit from better employees and having all or some of their costs subsidized. Employees receive assistance meeting their retirement goals, and the government winds up with a smaller burden to take care of an aging population.

FICA TIP CREDIT

This credit provides big benefits for businesses in the hospitality industry. Restaurants can receive a credit for Social Security and Medicare tax paid on tips, which are in excess of the federal minimum wage. The credit is 7.65 percent of the reported eligible tips.

INVESTMENT TAX CREDIT

The investment tax credit is like the business version of the energy efficient home improvement credit and residential clean energy credit. Individuals can also take advantage of this credit as long as it's used for business property.

The main item that would apply for most businesses is energy systems—specifically solar. You can receive a credit of up to 30 percent of the costs of installing solar on business property, including rental real estate. And you can add to this huge benefit because you can still depreciate a significant portion of the investment despite taking the credit. You should include the value of the credit and the depreciation deductions in determining the after-tax cost of these improvements.

RESEARCH AND DEVELOPMENT CREDIT

Research and development is good for society. At least that's what the government has decided, and I can't say I disagree. Companies can receive a tax credit for certain costs associated with research and development, including design, development or improvement, processes, techniques, formulas, or software.

Conclusion

I've listed only some of the most common and most beneficial credits here as a reference because I want you to understand how tax credits work and that there are many credits out there that you could use to reduce your tax burden.

There's a good chance that you have qualified for a tax credit at some point whether you realized it or not. Credits are not something you want to miss out on, so you should talk with your tax advisor to see if there might be some tax credits that could benefit you or your business.

Remember the idea that creating value for the community can lower your tax bill and try to look at value from the government's point of view. That value can come in the form of children (literally the future of the country), or lower energy usage, or more money in retirement accounts, or a more educated population. If you think you or your business is creating or enhancing something of societal value, check for a tax credit that you might use.

Chapter Summary

✓ *Tax credits can tell you what the government values the most.*

✓ *A tax credit is typically better than a tax deduction.*

✓ *A deduction is similar to a discount.*

✓ *Some credits are refundable, while others are not.*

✓ *Some—but not all—credits can be carried forward to a future year if not fully utilized.*

✓ *Tax credits for individuals will typically be reduced based on income levels, while business tax credits do not usually phase out based on income levels.*

6

LOOK BEFORE YOU LEAP: WHICH BUSINESS ENTITY IS BEST FOR YOU?

You've decided to pursue a new business venture. You've put a lot of time and energy into creating an idea and studying best practices, but now it's time to get cracking on the details. When it comes to tax savings, your single most impactful decision is probably your business structure.

Mark my words—you do not want to skip this part of the planning phase. I've seen entire tax plans fail because someone didn't do the proper research, didn't seek out advice from a professional, or looked for the cheapest source rather than the most reliable source. The cost of skimping on this step often ends up far greater than the time or money you would have spent on getting it right the first time.

The first important detail to understand is that a legal entity, often created by state statute, is not synonymous with the tax entities recognized by the IRS. A legal entity for state purposes can be treated by the IRS in different ways depending on how it's organized or the elections you make. It's also possible that a legal entity can be completely ignored for tax purposes. Let's start by identifying the most common legal entities and then discussing how they can or will be treated for tax purposes.

For federal tax purposes, there are four types of business entities that all have their own special tax rules and treatment: **sole proprietorships, C-corporations, S-corporations,** and **partnerships.** Notice that these entity types recognized by the IRS do not match up with many common state entities, as you can see in Figure 6.1. Once you have created a legal entity, you must determine how the IRS will treat that entity for tax purposes and whether you could or should make an election to treat that entity differently.

Figure 6.1. State legal entities often do not exactly parallel IRS designations.

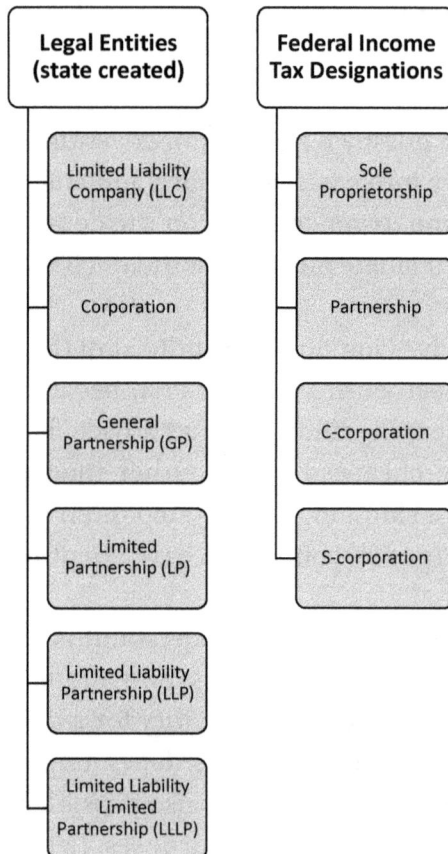

Legal Entities (state created)	Federal Income Tax Designations
Limited Liability Company (LLC)	Sole Proprietorship
Corporation	Partnership
General Partnership (GP)	C-corporation
Limited Partnership (LP)	S-corporation
Limited Liability Partnership (LLP)	
Limited Liability Limited Partnership (LLLP)	

TAX TENET #11

Time is of the essence. Don't waste it when it comes to planning.

Sole Proprietorships

Sole proprietorships are those entities with a single owner that are taxed to individuals at their applicable tax rates. These are often the easiest to create because they don't require any legal formation to start, although you can choose to have a legal entity for protection.

The tax rate of your sole proprietorship will depend on other income reported on your individual income tax return (i.e., your marginal tax brackets). Not only will you pay tax at the individual income tax rates, but your sole proprietorship income will be subject to the 15.3 percent self-employment tax up to the applicable limit for that year ($168,600 for tax year 2024). A salary to the owner does not need to be paid as all the income is taxed to the owner already. Any income or cash removed from the company will not be subject to tax since the income is already taxed when earned to the individual.

IT GOES HERE

Sole proprietorships will report their business activity on Form 1040, Schedule C.

The greatest benefit of sole proprietorships is the ease at which they are created, as you can see in Figure 6.2. But because they are so easy to create, they are generally subject to more abuse by taxpayers. This means the IRS will often scrutinize these businesses more heavily to determine whether reported expenses are truly deductible or whether the sole proprietorship is even a business for tax purposes in the first place. Sole proprietorships are by far the most commonly audited type of entity.

You can have a sole proprietorship without creating a legal entity and simply start doing business, or you can create an LLC with you as the sole member. Most will choose to create an LLC for legal purposes, but remember to check the rules of your state and local tax structures. This can also help you look and act more like a true business in the eyes of the government.

IN CASE OF AUDIT

Make sure any business bank accounts are in the name of the LLC or in the business name, if operating as a DBA (Doing Business As). You'll want to run all business income and expenses through this account. Avoid running personal expenditures through this account.

Even if you are armed with the knowledge of which expenses are truly deductible and how to best document those expenses, you would probably prefer to avoid the mental and financial drain of an audit. Another drawback to a sole proprietorship is your lack of ability to plan for reducing self-employment tax as all of the entity's income will be subject to this tax, up to the Social Security limits for that year.

Figure 6.2. Creating a sole proprietorship

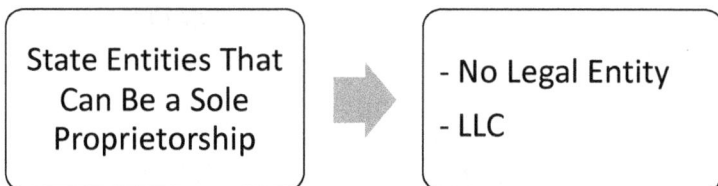

State Entities That Can Be a Sole Proprietorship ➡ - No Legal Entity - LLC

C-corporations

The popularity of corporations has waned greatly in the last few decades because of the creation of **limited liability companies (LLCs).** But if you are thinking about setting up your business as a corporation be clear about whether you choose a C-corporation or an S-corporation. They are taxed very differently.

C-corporations have become less common because of the double taxation nature that corporations face. The income earned by a corporation will be taxed at the corporate tax rate, currently a flat 21 percent. Once the income is distributed to its owners, the income will be taxed again to the individuals as a dividend. The tax rate to the individual on the dividend will depend on a variety of factors, but generally it will be 15–20 percent.

Corporations can have a single owner or multiple owners, and the officers of the corporation, which are many times also shareholders, will receive a salary. The salary is deducted by the corporation to reduce the corporate tax and therefore also the dividend tax. However, the salary will be taxed to the individual receiving the compensation and will be subject to the same tax rates as compensation from any other employer. This means tax will be paid on the salary at the individual marginal tax rates and subject to self-employment tax.

The reasons to organize your business as a C-corporation are few and far between. Typically, you would only choose this entity for very specific reasons. One would be to gain the qualified small business stock exclusion, which essentially allows some or all the gain from the sale of the corporation to be tax-free if certain conditions are met. This **tax exclusion** is only going to make sense for a select few businesses given the other negatives associated with corporations. For most business ventures, you can write off a C-corporation as a possible business structure.

In addition to the potential for high taxes due to the double taxed nature, there are many other negatives to consider. From a logistical standpoint, corporations are often difficult to form and dissolve without negative tax consequences. It can be difficult to bring new shareholders into a corporation as shareholders would often benefit much more from entering a partnership. Overall, a corporation lacks flexibility and in 99 percent or more of cases will not provide any tax benefits over the other options.

Should you and your CPA decide that a C-corporation is best for your business, you can create a corporation or LLC with the state, as shown in Figure 6.3. A corporation will be taxed as a C-corporation by default. If you create an LLC, you will need to make sure you make the election to be taxed as a C-corporation because this will not be the default. Most commonly, an LLC that makes an election to be taxed as a C-corporation will be used because there are fewer annual reporting requirements for an LLC. You'll want to include your local business attorney when you decide which option is best for your business.

IT GOES HERE

The activity of a C-corporation is reported on Form 1120. Dividends paid by the corporation are reported on Form 1099-DIV.

Figure 6.3. Creating a C-corporation

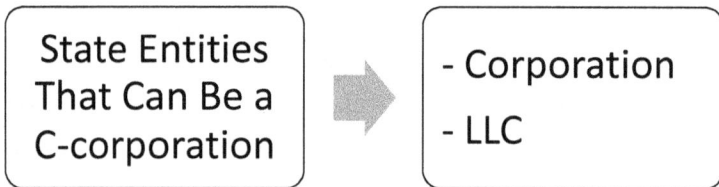

| State Entities That Can Be a C-corporation | ⇒ | - Corporation
- LLC |

S-corporations

I frequently get asked about S-corporations. A lot of people seem to think that an S-corporation is some magical entity that allows deductions not given to other entities. There are advantages to S-corporations, but not nearly as many as people seem to believe.

An S-corporation is often referred to as a "flow-through" entity because income from the organization will not be taxed at the entity level but will "flow through" to the individual and be taxed at individual income tax rates. Notice that this is similar to a sole proprietorship.

A key difference is that the income passing through the S-corporation is not subject to self-employment tax. However, the government requires S-corporations to pay a "reasonable salary" to its shareholders, and this salary is subject to the self-employment tax as well as individual income tax. No matter how you structure your business, the government still expects you to pay your "fair share" of self-employment tax.

IN CASE OF AUDIT

Make sure to determine a reasonable salary for any shareholders of the S-corporation. This is a highly audited item for S-corporation owners because many will pay low or even no salaries to avoid the self-employment taxes. The self-employment tax game is about not paying more than your fair share, not completely disregarding it when it's owed.

Even though S-corporations can potentially provide a better solution for self-employment tax than sole proprietorships can, they still leave a lot to be desired. In fact, the S-corporation's reasonable salary requirement eliminates the self-employment tax benefit for many potential owners. A reasonable salary is based on what a person in the same job as yours would earn in an arm's-length transaction. To determine a reasonable salary, you must consider whether you are the sole contributor to the income or if other employees or capital investments generate a portion. If you are the sole contributor, it is difficult to say all the income from the S-corporation should be anything other than your salary—which would make all the income subject to the self-employment tax.

Similar to a C-corporation, you can create either a corporation or an LLC with the state; see Figure 6.4. Again, if you choose to create an LLC, you'll need to make sure the election to be taxed as an S-corporation is made, as this will not be the default. You will also need to make an election to treat a corporation as an S-corporation for tax purposes.

To S-corp or Not To S-corp

Morgan, a web designer, decides to start her own business because she is tired of dealing with her boss, who won't listen to her ideas. She sets up an S-corporation, Morgan's Web Designs (MWD), that quickly attracts plenty of clients and generates $100,000 of gross receipts in the first year. MWD racks up $20,000 of deductions, leaving a net taxable income of $80,000. Morgan has no employees, and her web design services generate all of the income for MWD.

A market survey of web designers in the area shows salaries ranging from $50,000 to $120,000, depending on experience and other factors. Because MWD's net income of $80,000 falls within the typical range of employees performing web design and because the only activity generating the income is Morgan's service, the IRS will probably expect that most, if not all, of the income from MWD should be disbursed as salary to Morgan. It would be difficult for Morgan to make a different case. If all MWD income is paid to Morgan as a salary, she will pay self-employment tax on all the income, so there would be little advantage to setting up MWD as an S-corporation rather than a sole proprietorship, although the S-corporation does potentially carry a lower audit risk.

On the other hand, if Morgan hired some employees to expand MWD's capacity, there is more potential for avoiding self-employment tax. If MWD earned a net income of $200,000 with employees, Morgan could pay herself a reasonable salary of $80,000, according to market surveys. This would mean the remaining net income of the business, $120,000, would escape self-employment tax.

Figure 6.4. Creating an S-corporation

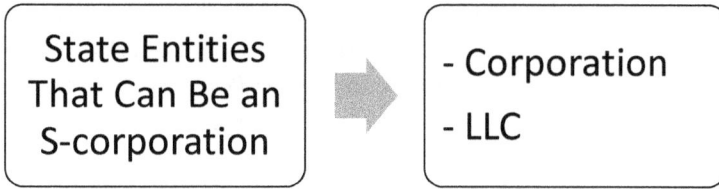

BEWARE

You should avoid using a C-corporation or an S-corporation to own real estate in almost all circumstances.

IT GOES HERE

The activity of an S-corporation is reported on Form 1120-S.

Partnerships

I typically recommend my clients establish a business with more than one owner as a partnership. Similar to S-corporations, partnerships are considered a flow-through entity, and all the income, deductions, and credits are reported at the partnership level. A partnership will file a separate tax return from its owners, and each partner will be entitled to their share of the activity from the partnership. The income and deductions will be taxed at the partner's tax rates.

STRATEGY TIP

The guaranteed payment for partnerships is the equivalent of a salary in an S-corporation. A guaranteed payment is an amount not based on the income earned by the company that is paid to a partner. It is very similar to a salary in that it is subject to self-employment taxes for the partner who receives it. However, there is no requirement that a partnership must make a guaranteed payment, unlike the requirement for a reasonable salary in an S-corporation.

Figure 6.5 details the three main reasons I prefer partnerships over the other entity choices available. There are a variety of state-created entities that are taxed as partnerships, and each of them carry their own advantages and disadvantages. Talk to your advisor to determine which is best for your situation.

Figure 6.5. Partnerships offer benefits over other entities.

Audits	• Audit risk is extremely low.
Lower Taxes	• Generally results in the lowest tax. • Benefits from preferential capital gain rates. • Losses from partnerships can offset your other income since it's "flow through." Limitations may apply. • Does not establish double tax. • Offers opportunity to avoid self-employment tax.
Flexibility	• Offers most flexibility. • Easily add and remove assets without tax consequences. • Offers way to specially allocate income and loss to partners. • Switch partners with no adverse consequences in most cases.

IT GOES HERE

The activity of a partnership is reported on Form 1065.

STRATEGY TIP

Although S-corporations are often touted as the solution to overpaying in self-employment taxes, you can accomplish the same thing with the correct structure in a partnership.

Figure 6.6. Creating a partnership

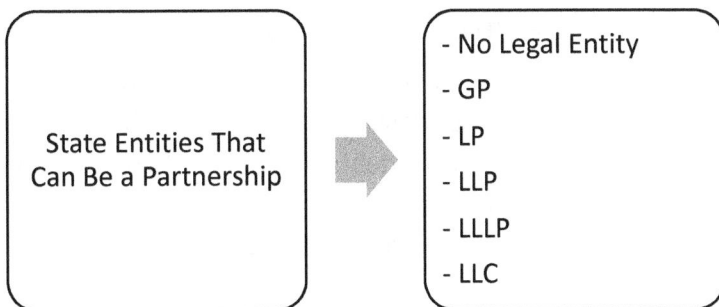

State Entities That Can Be a Partnership

- No Legal Entity
- GP
- LP
- LLP
- LLLP
- LLC

As shown in Figure 6.6, you can form a partnership without a legal entity by acting as a partnership in practice or by creating a *general partnership, limited partnership, limited liability partnership, limited liability limited partnership,* or *limited liability company.* The limited liability company (LLC) is by far the most common. We'll go over some of the key characteristics for each of these options, but make sure to involve your CPA and attorney before you set anything up.

TAX TENET #12

Flexibility is king.

GENERAL PARTNERSHIP (GP)

These are formed with two or more partners, all of whom will be considered *general partners.* You will want to avoid this structure most of the time since general partners do not have limited liability. That means a creditor could go after the assets of the general partnership *and* the assets of the general partners themselves.

LIMITED PARTNERSHIP (LP)

A limited partnership will have two or more partners, but this structure requires at least one general partner and one *limited partner.* The general partners could be subject to the liabilities of the partnership, while a limited partner generally is not.

LIMITED LIABILITY PARTNERSHIP (LLP)

In this format, partners are generally not liable for the debts of the partnership or the other partners. It is possible, however, that a partner could become liable for debts personally through negligence or something similar. LLPs will generally have more annual reporting requirements than an LLC (see discussion below), depending on the state in which it is created. A potential benefit of the LLP is that all the partners will typically have the same management responsibilities. Due to the management structure, LLPs are most commonly used by professionals such as accountants and attorneys but are generally not the first choice for most businesses.

LIMITED LIABILITY LIMITED PARTNERSHIP (LLLP)

This entity is considered a hybrid of the limited partnership and the limited liability partnership. In this structure, you will have at least one general partner and at least one limited partner, similar to an LP. However, unlike in an LP, the general partner will generally not be subject to the debts of the partnership. This is an attractive entity if you still need a general partner from a management perspective with limited partners who will not be involved in the management, but the LLC is still the entity of choice for most organizations.

LIMITED LIABILITY COMPANY (LLC)

All right—we finally get to my favorite entity for most businesses or even for personal assets. LLCs combine the best of all the entities above without the pitfalls. Unlike the other partnership entities, there is no general partner or limited partner. Instead, LLCs are organized with managers and members.

The manager is similar to a general partner in that they will be the one who manages the day-to-day of the entity. The difference between a manager in an LLC and a general partner in one of the other partnership arrangements is that the LLC manager will not be liable for the debts of the partnership.

LLC members are the ones with actual ownership in the entity. Members don't have to be involved in the day-to-day management, may have voting powers for major decisions, and are not liable for the debts of the partnership. Unlike limited partners in the other entities, a member can also be a manager. And a manager can be a member but does not have to be.

A key difference between all the other entity types described in the partnership discussion is that an LLC does not require two owners. This benefit makes it much more flexible than the other partnership types. You need a manager and a member, but the single member can also be the manager.

One of my favorite aspects of the LLC is that it can be recognized as any federal entity type depending on the number of owners and elections that are made, which makes it the most flexible entity type by far from a federal tax perspective. However, because there are a wide variety of available tax treatments, it's important to understand the default tax treatments, shown in Table 6.1, before trying to understand other aspects.

An LLC with one owner will by default be treated as a "disregarded entity" for federal tax purposes. This means the LLC activity will be reported on the tax return of the owner as if the LLC does not exist. This does not prevent the LLC from maintaining its legal treatment; it is simply a federal (and usually state) tax determination only. An LLC with two or more owners will by default be treated as a partnership for federal tax purposes.

Regardless of the number of owners, an LLC can elect to be taxed as either an S-corporation or a C-corporation for federal tax purposes. Generally, if you want an entity to be taxed as an S-corporation you should set it up as an LLC and make the election.

Table 6.1. Default LLC tax treatments

Number of Members	Default Treatment	Available Elections
One	Disregarded entity	S-corporation or C-corporation
Two or More	Partnership	S-corporation or C-corporation

While the information in this chapter provides a general overview of the different entities that could be treated as a partnership for federal tax purposes, be sure to discuss your options with an attorney located in the state where you create the entity and where you operate the business—if different. Each state has its own laws that govern the legalities and management of the entity. See Table 6.2 for a reminder of the correct form to use for each tax entity and Table 6.3 for a comparison of the various tax entities based on what we've covered. You will see partnerships rank well in all the relevant categories.

Table 6.2. Form guide for tax entities

Guide For Correct Form To Use	
Sole Proprietorship	Schedule C (Form 1040)
C-corporation	Form 1120
S-corporation	Form 1120-S
Partnership	Form 1065

⚠️ **BEWARE**

Most states follow the federal tax treatment of business entities when levying state taxes. However, many states require a separate tax filing for certain entities and attach a fee. For example, California requires annual LLC reports to pay an annual fee in addition to the partnership filing for California. Pay attention to these additional state filing and fee requirements when choosing your business structure.

Table 6.3. Comparison of each tax entity

	Sole Proprietorship	**C-corporation**	**S-corporation**	**Partnership**
Self-employment tax avoidance	None	Some	High	High
Flexibility	Medium	Low	Low	High
Tax rates	Individual tax rates	Double tax	Individual tax rates	Individual tax rates
Legal entity	None or LLC	LLC or corporation	LLC or corporation	Many
Audit risk	High	Medium	Medium	Extremely low

Independent Contractors vs. Employees

In addition to choosing your best business structure, many businesses will have to decide between hiring ***independent contractors*** and/or employees at some point, especially if they plan to grow. For tax purposes and ease of paperwork, most employers would typically prefer to hire more independent contractors and fewer employees.

The benefit of independent contractors over employees is the employer is not responsible for paying self-employment taxes or withholding any federal and state income taxes from the contractors' paychecks. You can simply decide what amount to pay the contractor and submit those payments as agreed. The independent contractor would be responsible for making any income tax payments and paying 100 percent of the self-employment tax.

> **IN CASE OF AUDIT**
>
> *Make sure to have all independent contractors fill out a Form W-9. If you do not receive this form or the contractor is a nonresident alien, you are required to withhold taxes from the payments. If you pay a contractor $600 or more during a tax year, you must send them a 1099-MISC or 1099-NEC at the end of the year.*

It might seem obvious that a business should utilize only independent contractors instead of employees. However, the IRS says if you exercise a certain amount of control of the work being performed by the individual you have hired, you must characterize them as an employee. This can sometimes be a blurry line and is often based on the facts and circumstances of the situation.

Here are the most common factors to consider when determining whether the person you're paying to do work for your business is an independent contractor or an employee.

- How much control does the business have over the right to direct and control when and how work is completed?
- Does the worker have unreimbursed business expenses?
- Does the worker provide their own tools or facilities for performing the work?
- Does the worker perform services for other individuals or businesses?
- How is the worker paid (i.e., hourly, salary, or per job)?

- Can the worker have a profit or loss? Does the worker have expenses the business is not responsible for?
- What written or oral agreements describe the relationship between the business and the worker?
- Does the worker receive any benefits from the business, such as insurance, retirement, vacation pay, etc.?
- How permanent is the relationship?
- How critical are the worker's services to the company's regular business?

These factors are considered as a whole, so no single criteria will be the determining factor. If possible for your business, you will generally want to avoid giving the employee classification to as many workers as possible. This may even be to the benefit of the worker as well. Although independent contractors are responsible for all self-employment taxes, they may also be eligible for the 20 percent pass-through deduction; see the discussion on the qualified business income deduction in Chapter 7. Everyone likes a win-win situation, right?

IN CASE OF AUDIT

Document the reasons why you have decided to pay someone as an independent contractor instead of an employee. This is a highly audited area of the tax code.

STRATEGY TIP

Individuals who provide a service to a business should have their own CPA analyze the advantages and disadvantages of the Qualified Business Income Deduction described in Chapter 7 and the self-employment tax burden when deciding whether to work as an independent contractor or employee.

Chapter Summary

✓ *The type of entity you choose for your business is one of the most critical decisions and will determine how the business is taxed.*

✓ *There is a difference between the legal entity and the federal income tax designations of entities.*

✓ *Sole proprietorships tend to have the highest audit rates.*

✓ *Partnerships tend to have the lowest audit rates.*

✓ *Partnerships tend to be the most flexible entities from a tax perspective.*

✓ *Self-employment tax considerations are an important part of your entity choice.*

✓ *Put careful consideration into whether you hire workers as independent contractors or employees.*

7

WHERE THERE'S A WILL, THERE'S A WRITE-OFF

"Don't I receive more deductions if I'm an S-corporation?"

I hear that question a lot, and I have to tell people that it's a misconception. Frankly, I blame the accounting profession for that misconception because so many accounting professionals encourage taxpayers to structure as an S-corporation.

The reality is a business can receive the same deductions regardless of its entity type. (That's true for the most part; there are always exceptions, you know.) Now, the mechanics of how a specific entity can take those deductions will vary, but the net effect is usually the same.

The most important criteria for tax deductions—regardless of entity type—are whether they are "ordinary and necessary." This is how deductions for all businesses are judged. We will talk about some deductions that require additional support in the next chapter, but "ordinary and necessary" will cover 90 percent of your potential deductions.

Okay, ordinary and necessary, what the heck does that mean? Well, ordinary refers to whether or not the expense is common and accepted in your specific line of business. For example, a musician could deduct the cost of purchasing music scores, music equipment, microphones, and other similar items. However, such purchases would not be ordinary for a general contractor. Therefore, those items could be deductible for a musician, but not a contractor.

Necessary refers to whether the expense is necessary—or appropriate—for your business. For example, an attorney will need a computer to send emails, draft documents, perform research, and handle other tasks. However, attorneys probably don't need the highest-end computer with the best graphics to perform those tasks. But what if that attorney is also a big gamer? Well, a computer that costs many times more than necessary for office work would not be considered necessary—even if the attorney wants to use it for gaming after work.

As you can see, expenses may be deductible for one business but not another. As long as your expenses meet "ordinary and necessary" criteria, they will most likely be allowed. Most businesses will be able to take deductions for office supplies, legal and accounting services, employee and owner salaries, independent contractor fees, insurance, utilities, rent, professional dues, advertising, employee benefits, and much more.

Now let's look at some common deductions that you may not ordinarily consider and that carry some special guidelines.

Qualified Business Income Deduction

The **qualified business income deduction (QBID)** is a relatively new deduction that was created as part of the 2017 Tax Cuts and Jobs Act. This is what I call a freebie or "fake" deduction. Fake deductions are those that do not correspond with a cash or economic outflow. These are the best deductions—they're freebies—and who doesn't like a freebie?

The QBID is calculated as 20 percent of the qualified income from a qualifying trade or business. This is where the QBID earns the nickname "20% pass-through deduction." The QBID is limited at certain income levels and completely disallowed at higher incomes for these businesses:

- Health

- Law

- Accounting

- Actuarial science

- Performing arts

- Consulting

- Athletics

- Financial services

- Brokerage services

- Any trade or business where the principal asset is the reputation or skill of one or more of its employees (typically endorsements).

Businesses that do not belong in the above categories may still find the QBID limited at higher income levels. The income levels are inflation-adjusted each year, so you'll want to keep up with them. If you're above the phaseout levels, the limitations in Figure 7.1 apply to each business activity separately.

Figure 7.1. Limitations for higher income taxpayers

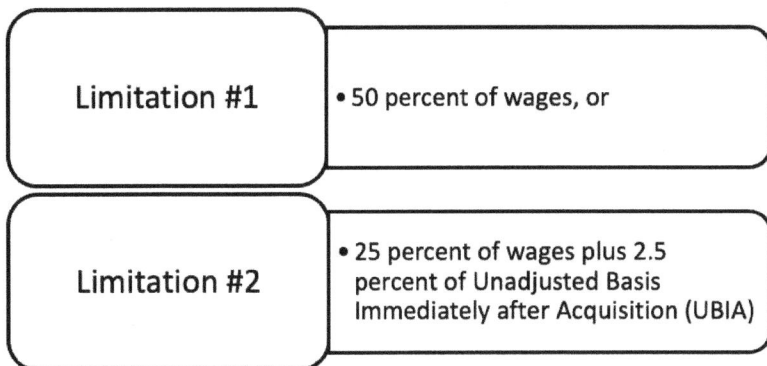

Limitation #1	• 50 percent of wages, or
Limitation #2	• 25 percent of wages plus 2.5 percent of Unadjusted Basis Immediately after Acquisition (UBIA)

STRATEGY TIP

There is an option to group similar businesses for purposes of the limitations in Figure 7.1. This can be especially helpful if you have one business with all the wages paid from it and another related entity without wages. The business without wages may not receive a QBID, but by aggregating the businesses together, you can get a QBID for both.

A major factor in determining whether your business will be eligible for the QBID is the type of income earned, as should be evident in the previous list. It's also important to understand that salaries and wages earned as an employee are not eligible for the deduction, and that includes salaries paid to an S-corporation owner. The only portion of the S-corporation owner's income that would be eligible for the QBID is the portion that is flow-through income in excess of their salary, which should further incentivize owners to take a lower salary. (Remember, however, that you cannot avoid paying a "reasonable salary," so be careful.) The partnership equivalent of a salary, guaranteed payments, are not eligible for this deduction, but the flow-through income in excess of the guaranteed payment would be eligible.

In addition, there are certain types of income earned by a business that already receive lower tax rates than the typical ordinary income earned by a business, such as capital gains. These will not be eligible for the QBID. The deduction will generally be applied only to ordinary business income and rental income that is taxed at ordinary tax rates.

The business structure is also an important factor in determining eligibility for the QBID because it is only available for business income that is taxed on an individual taxpayer's tax return. In other words, C-corporations, which report and pay tax separately from the individual owners, are not eligible for this deduction—yet another reason to avoid a C-corporation structure. Income earned by a sole proprietorship would be eligible for the deduction, in addition to the pass-through income from partnerships and S-corporations.

There's a lot of detail packed into this deduction, but you'll be missing out if you don't try to figure it out. Never give up a fake deduction.

To help illustrate how the QBID applies in different business structures, let's run through some examples, which are shown in Table 7.1. For simplicity, we will assume none of the limitations described above apply and that you are in the 24 percent marginal tax bracket.

Table 7.1. QBID Examples with salaries

	Sole Proprietorship	S-corporation	Partnership
Gross income	$200,000	$200,000	$200,000
Expenses	$50,000	$50,000	$50,000
Salary to owner*	NA	$50,000	NA
Guaranteed payment to owner*	NA	NA	$50,000
Net income	$150,000	$100,000	$100,000
QBID: net income × 20 percent	$30,000	$20,000	$20,000
Taxable income: net income minus QBID	$120,000	$80,000	$80,000
Tax savings	$7,200 ($30,000 QBID × 24 percent marginal tax rate)	$4,800 ($20,000 QBID × 24 percent marginal tax rate)	$4,800 ($20,000 QBID × 24 percent marginal tax rate)

*Not eligible for deduction

In Table 7.1, you can see that the owner of the sole proprietorship and the owner of the S-corporation are taking home the same income. The sole proprietor is netting $150,000 from the business and the S-corporation owner is netting $100,000 plus their $50,000 salary. However, since the salary is not eligible for the QBID, the tax savings for the sole proprietor is greater. Of course, looking only at the QBID will not allow for a full analysis of the self-employment tax differences between these two business structures. Doesn't it look fun to be a tax advisor who needs to balance all of these overlapping factors before giving tax advice about business decisions!?

STRATEGY TIP

The salary paid to an owner of an S-corporation is not eligible for the QBID. However, by operating as a sole proprietorship, all of the income will be subject to self-employment tax. You might actually be better as a sole proprietorship subject to self-employment tax who is also eligible for this deduction on all the income from the business. Your CPA should be able to help you perform this analysis to see whether the trade-off for higher self-employment taxes makes up for a larger QBID.

You can also see in Table 7.1 the deduction for a partnership is the same as the S-corporation example. However, you can easily increase the benefits in a partnership by not making a guaranteed payment. Unlike an S-corporation, which requires a reasonable salary to be paid, there is no requirement to make a guaranteed payment in a partnership structure. You could instead allow the guaranteed payment to be included in the net income of the business, which would make the deduction similar to the sole proprietor's. See why I love partnerships so much? The flexibility of a partnership is unmatched by any of the other entity structures.

QBID FOR RENTAL ACTIVITIES

Even people who don't run their own business may be able to take advantage of the QBID because it is available for rental real estate. The rental activity must be considered a trade or business to benefit, which most are, so it's easier to describe the circumstances when real estate does *not* rise to that level. Rental activities will generally not be eligible for the QBID in the following circumstances.

- Rental property that is comprised of triple net leases.

- Rental property leased to family or friends. The IRS doesn't believe you own the rental property for the purposes of profit if you lease it to someone close to you.

- Rental property with long, unexplained vacancies, which is another indication to the IRS that you are not engaged in the rental activity for profit.

- Rental activities where the landlord is not scheduling for repairs, advertising for leases, etc. An example of this would be a single-family home where the tenant schedules repairs and requests reimbursement from the landlord. Hiring a property manager who performs these functions would not prevent the rental activity from being eligible for the deduction.

STRATEGY TIP

If you invest in syndicated real estate or real estate partnerships, the trade or business deduction is made at the real estate activity level. In other words, you do not need to actively or materially participate in the rental activity for it to qualify for the QBID as long as it's still considered a trade or business.

Start-up Expenses

If you're starting or acquiring a new business, **start-up expenses** will be a big part of your process. That's why it's important to know the rules about deducting start-up expenses from your taxes.

A few years ago, one of my clients was a restaurant owner who was opening a new restaurant location and concept. If you've ever been in the restaurant business, you know there are a lot of expenses before you earn your first dollar. My client incurred expenses for training employees, purchasing silverware and furniture, creating a menu design, and many other items. All expenses occurred before the opening of the restaurant were considered start-up expenses.

Any new business would face similar start-up costs. If you're acquiring an existing business, the costs to investigate that business would also be considered start-up costs.

Start-up expenses are subject to a specific IRS rule: you can take a deduction for up to $5,000 of any start-up expenses (necessary outlays before your doors open or you earn your first dollar in sales) in the first year you open or acquire a business. But start-up expenses in excess of $5,000 must be deducted over time—fifteen years to be specific. However, once your total start-up expenses exceed $50,000, the amount you can deduct in the first year is limited dollar for dollar by the amount that exceeds $50,000.

For example, if your start-up costs for a business are $52,000, you can only deduct $3,000 in the first year of opening your doors. The $5,000 deduction is reduced by $2,000 because your start-up expenses exceeded $50,000 by that amount. The remaining $49,000 is deducted evenly over a period of fifteen years. If you have $55,000 or more of start-up expenses, there will be no first-year deduction; all your start-up costs must be deducted evenly over fifteen years.

BEWARE

The actual cost of purchasing a business is not considered a start-up cost. The deductibility of purchasing a business will depend on a variety of factors.

....

Good News, Bad News

My client John spent hundreds of thousands of dollars investigating the possibility of starting a new business, even as I warned him to keep his costs as low as possible. After a few years, John decided the new business idea was not going to work—after he had incurred about $300,000 of expenses.

John called me up one afternoon, glum about giving up his business dream and wondering whether he could deduct all his costs even though he never opened the business.

Since I knew John was already down, I decided to tell him the good news first. "Yes, all of those expenses are deductible now," I said.

John was ecstatic, until I told him the bad news. Although, the costs were deductible, they would be characterized as capital losses, not ordinary deductions. As we discussed in Chapter 3, capital losses can offset other capital gains or a maximum of $3,000 each year of other income.

Obviously, John wasn't happy to hear about that limitation, so our next task was to figure out how to generate some capital gains that John could use to offset these losses. Luckily for John, he had been thinking about selling a real estate investment anyway. If he sold the real estate asset, it would generate enough capital gains to fully deduct his start-up expenses.

Finally, there was a silver lining to John's failed business dilemma: no tax on his real estate investment.

....

IN CASE OF AUDIT

Large capital losses carry a higher risk of audit. Don't think because the business failed that you should not keep these records to substantiate your write-off.

STRATEGY TIP

Often, timing is everything when it comes to taxes. If there's a chance of having a failed business with lots of start-up costs, you should start planning ahead for ways to minimize the loss. Make sure you talk to your tax advisor before you make decisions.

Organizational Expenses

Start-up costs likely aren't the only type of expense you will incur when starting a new business. You'll also have the costs of creating the legal entity in the form of filing and creating operating or other agreements for the business. These are considered **organizational expenses.**

The rules for organizational expenses follow the same rules as start-up expenses. That is, you can deduct up to $5,000 of organizational costs in the year your business begins, except for instances where your organizational costs exceed $50,000. Most of the time costs for organizing a business won't exceed $5,000, so they are generally fully deductible in the first year.

STRATEGY TIP

Make sure you keep track of your organizational expenses separate from your start-up costs. This will allow a deduction of up to $10,000 in the first year for both combined (up to $5,000 each) and may prevent some of the expenses from being disallowed due to the $50,000 limit.

Chapter Summary

✓ *You generally receive the same business deductions regardless of entity type.*

✓ *The QBID is available for most businesses, but you need to be aware of certain businesses where this deduction is limited or not allowed.*

✓ *You can use the aggregation election to maximize your QBID when there are multiple businesses.*

✓ *You need to determine whether you should maximize your self-employment tax savings or the QBID.*

✓ *You should track your start-up expenses and organizational expenses separately to maximize your deductions for these.*

✓ *Advance tax planning should take place whenever you decide to shut down a start-up business.*

8

LET THE GOVERNMENT PAY
FOR YOUR LIFESTYLE

In the early pages of this book, I told you employees tend to receive the fewest tax breaks. In other words, employees tend to pay the highest rate of tax as they have fewer tax incentives available for them.

A way to increase your tax benefits is to start your own small business. Think about it, we all have hobbies, activities, or ideas we enjoy. You likely also have a lot of knowledge from simply being an employee and learning from an existing company or individuals within that company. Nothing in the tax code prevents you from starting your own business while you hold on to the safety of your recurring paycheck. In fact, many—if not most—self-employed entrepreneurs start establishing their business while they still work for someone else.

As a business owner, you will likely be providing society with some essential needs the government will perceive as important. This could be offering employment, or critical services and products, and—of course—generating more revenue that the government can tax. Yes, if you receive income from your business, it will likely be subject to tax, but even after taxes, you will still pocket more cash than you would receive without the business. As a result of creating a business that adds additional value to society, you can often convert what would have been personal expenses (and therefore nondeductible) into deductible business expenses. Remember in Chapter 2 we discussed above the line deductions? The deductions for businesses are above the line, which benefits you as the taxpayer.

TAX TENET #13

Businesses reap the most tax benefits.

In previous chapters, we discussed some of the most common deductions allowed for most businesses. In this chapter, we're going to dive into what I refer to as **lifestyle deductions.** Now don't get me wrong, all business expenses must meet the ordinary and necessary test. Just setting yourself up as a "business owner," isn't some get-out-of-jail-free card allowing you to do whatever you want. However, when you know the rules, you can effectively get the government to subsidize your lifestyle.

Chapters 6 and 7 provide more information about how you can get started with your own business and what kind of tax credits and deductions may be available to a business. In this chapter, we will discuss how having your own business will unlock many deductions not available to you previously. These deductions, if planned correctly, can be used to reduce your other sources of income so you will pay lower taxes. Starting a business allows you to legitimately convert nondeductible personal expenditures into tax deductions. Many of the deductions that I will describe in this chapter are expenses you may incur already as an employee, but you can reap nice tax savings by thinking of them in the context of a business. The possibilities for tax deductions as an employee are not nearly as consequential as those for businesses.

From Killing Weeds to Finding Savings

I started my career in public accounting with an almighty regular paycheck. (I'm rolling my eyes as I write this.) But I always had an interest in real estate, partly because I had grown up helping my father with his various rentals.

My fondest memories of the summer were being dropped off at one of his rentals early in the morning, armed with a cooler of water and some landscaping tools to attack the weeds in the backyard. I mean, the memories weren't fond at the time. This was one of those situations where your parents tell you, "One day you'll understand," and you don't believe them—until you actually do understand. I spent most summers and weekends watching my dad showing a property to prospective tenants, making repairs, driving around looking at property, and meeting tenants to collect monthly rent. I didn't appreciate it at the time, but I was learning the various ins and outs of property management and real estate ownership.

During college, I started reading books on personal finance and business, which of course led me to many books written on real estate. From these books I learned that a majority of independent wealthy people had achieved their financial success through real estate. And I realized that I already had firsthand experience in the business. (I don't know whether my father was intentionally trying to give me this experience, but I think he Mr. Miyagi'd me. Karate Kid fans know what I'm talking about, and yes, I'm making the name a verb.)

So real estate was the perfect business for me to start getting my feet wet as an entrepreneur. I already had the knowledge, the skill sets, and relevant experience. And I quickly discovered that in addition to all the specific tax advantages related to real estate, starting a real estate business allowed me to convert certain nondeductible personal expenses into deductible business expenses.

You see, after I bought my first rental property, I needed to lease it. In order to lease the property, I had to create a lease agreement and print it. Obviously, to create an agreement and print it, I needed a computer and a printer.

My personal computer was aging and balky, so I needed a new computer. If I had purchased a new computer to write letters to my dad and print out recipes, it would have been a personal expense and I could not have gained any tax benefit. But if I purchased a computer to create a lease agreement and print it out, it could be labeled as an ordinary and necessary business expense.

This was only the beginning. Having a real estate business also allowed me the potential for the home office deduction and auto-mobile deductions. These were expenses I was incurring regardless of having a business. Why not make them deductible?

The Government Will Subsidize Your Travel

As a CPA, I'm required to have a certain number of continuing education hours to renew my license. This is a common requirement among many professions. There are options for online courses and in-person courses, but I find I get a lot more out of the in-person courses as they require me to be present (mentally) and I can easily interact with the instructors and meet other like-minded professionals. These two benefits make it worthwhile to find the best in-person courses to attend, and sometimes the best courses are held outside of Tucson, Arizona, where I'm located.

Two very competent tax attorneys conduct the kind of classes I need to take multiple times throughout the year in different cities, so I chose to attend their session in Las Vegas. It just so happens that one of my favorite hobbies is playing poker, and Las Vegas has the best and biggest variety of poker rooms. But the main purpose of traveling to Las Vegas was the continuing education course, so all my travel expenses associated with the trip were deductible business expenses. This included the airfare from Tucson to Las

Vegas, the taxi ride from the airport to the hotel/casino where I was staying, my hotel costs, and the food I ate while I was there.

The classes took up most of the day, but when they ended late in the afternoon, my "vacation" would begin. As soon as I broke away from the classroom, I would find the closest poker room and rack up as many poker hours as possible. I couldn't deduct any poker losses, if there were any, because the poker was considered a personal expenditure, not related to my business. (Not to mention there are specific IRS rules for dealing with gambling winnings and losses.) However, I did get to deduct all travel expenses to do one of the things I love the most. I bet if you think hard enough you can find ways to pair a vacation with your business obligations. This is usually easy to do if you are required to travel for work.

The main test for whether business travel will be deductible is whether the principal purpose for the travel is for your trade or business. This means you can't simply choose to go on vacation, set up a meeting at that location, and call it deductible. You can, however, choose to travel to a location for a business reason, and while there, have some fun.

Keep in mind, the government is giving you a benefit, which means they expect one in return. The only reason it allows you to convert otherwise personal expenses into deductible business expenses is because you're providing value to society. In my case, the more educated I am on the latest tax laws, the more likely I am to give good advice and prepare taxes correctly for my clients. This ensures the government is getting paid, and it also means I can better advise my clients to take advantage of tax benefits they deserve. But don't worry, the government won't be losing out. Tax savings for my clients means they can reinvest their savings to grow their own businesses, invest in other endeavors, or maybe give to a charitable cause. This is all good for society.

STRATEGY TIP

Even if the travel is not considered primarily for business, you can still deduct the direct expenses related to your business during the trip. For example, if you attended a short conference while on your vacation, you could deduct the fees associated with registering for the conference.

SUBSTANTIATION REQUIREMENTS

Before we get into the specifics on how to maximize your business travel expenditures while mixing your trips with pleasure, let's discuss additional substantiation requirements. To be considered a valid travel expense in the eyes of the IRS, all of the expenses must be documented with the following:

- **The dates and locations of the trip.**
- **The business purposes of the travel.**
- **The amount and nature of each expense.**

Expenditures that are less than $75 do not have to be strictly documented, but I would still recommend keeping those receipts because if you're audited, the IRS will want to see support for your deductions. If you seem unprepared because you're missing a lot of receipts—even though the expenses may be under $75—your lack of documents could lead to even more scrutiny of the entire trip. The more documentation and evidence of your business purpose and associated expenses, the better you'll be.

IN CASE OF AUDIT

Documentation should be timely, meaning that you record it at the time of the expenditure and travel. A timely kept record will always carry more weight than a statement prepared later, which comes with the assumption that there will be a lack of accurate recall. Creating good habits when it comes to record-keeping will go far.

LOOKING FOR ADVANTAGES

Now that we've covered the mundane, but important, details of deducting travel expenses, we can discuss how to use these rules to your advantage. Recall, to be deductible, the principal purpose of the travel must be for business. This means if you need to fly to another state for a work conference, the associated expenses shown in Figure 8.1 will be deductible.

Figure 8.1. Expenses that can be deductible during business travel

Flights	Lodging	Car
Meals	Taxi/Uber	Parking
Telephone calls	Direct costs (registration fees)	Tips

We already know now the principal purpose test must be met for travel expenses. You also need to know that the travel must require you to sleep somewhere other than your tax home. I live in Tucson, Arizona, which is about two hours away from Phoenix, where I often travel to meet a client. If I come back the same day, I don't meet the sleep test so the trip would not be considered travel. This wouldn't prevent me from taking deductions for other items, such as auto expenses (discussed later) or business meals (discussed later), but I couldn't take travel expenses.

However, if I drive to Phoenix for a meeting on Tuesday and stay overnight for a meeting on Wednesday, I could consider this travel. It would make more sense to stay overnight in Phoenix for both meetings, making all my travel expenses deductible.

When you mix business travel with personal travel, you must allocate your expenses between the two to determine which amount is deductible. In the case of my business trips to Las Vegas for continuing education, if I have classes Thursday and Friday but decide to stay over the weekend for vacation, only my expenses for Thursday and Friday and my flights to and from Las Vegas would be deductible.

My expenses over the weekend would not be deductible since those would be considered nonbusiness days. A business day is one where your principal activity during business hours is in pursuit of your trade or business. Many consider principal to mean more than 50 percent of the working day. In other words, if you spend five hours out of an eight-hour working day on business, then the entire day is considered a business day.

Create a Business-Day Sandwich

I just said nonbusiness days on a business trip are not deductible. However, you can easily convert nonbusiness days into deductible business days if they fall between two business days. This counts for weekends and holidays too!

One year I attended a continuing education class in Las Vegas on a Thursday and Friday. Another continuing education class was scheduled for the next Monday through Wednesday. Because my Friday was a business day and my Monday was also a business day, I was able to count the weekend as business days. That means I could do anything I wanted on Saturday and Sunday and my hotel and meal expenses remained deductible. Although, if I had taken a cab ride to visit a friend over the weekend, the ride would be a nondeductible expense.

This is a great strategy to help subsidize the costs of some quick weekend vacations. In fact, if you're in the highest marginal tax bracket and a resident of a high tax state, like California, this could easily mean a 50 percent discount on your vacation expenses for the weekend. Not a bad deal!

FAMILY TIME

Many times you'll want to have friends or family accompany you on business trips if you know there will be some time for personal activities. Of course, the additional expenses for bringing those people along will not be deductible. If you're on a business trip and would need a single bed for yourself but you decide to spend an additional $50 a night to have two beds for your family member, the additional cost will not be a deductible business expense.

IN CASE OF AUDIT

If you are bringing friends or family on a business trip and those expenses are not deductible, be sure to have cost comparisons available to substantiate the deductible portion. For example, if you get a hotel room with two beds to bring a family member, have the receipt for the cost of the room, but also document what the cost of the room with one bed would have been. This is your deductible portion.

Of course, there are exceptions to that rule! You gotta love exceptions.

Although the travel for your spouse, friends, or children would generally not be deductible, the costs of their travel will be deductible if:

- The person is your employee;
- The person has a bona fide business purpose for the travel;
- The expense would otherwise be deductible.

So, hiring your spouse or making them your business partner or hiring your children can help make family vacations more affordable.

Remember, however, that the primary purpose must be business and everyone needs a bona fide business purpose for the travel. If your spouse does the accounting for your business but there is no bona fide business purpose for accountants to attend the new supplier conference in Hawaii, then their travel would not be deductible.

However, if your spouse attends an accounting refresher course while you are in your supplier meetings, then there would be a bona fide business purpose for his travel.

FOREIGN LANDS AND BIG BOATS

Most of the rules I've discussed in this chapter are specific to travel within the United States. There are different rules for deducting travel expenses when you go outside the United States, and they are typically more stringent.

You should also be aware that there are specific guidelines and limits to the amount of travel you can deduct for luxury water travel and cruise ships. You'll see a lot of people who are not tax professionals on social media claiming you can deduct business expenses for their conventions held on cruise ships. Make sure you check with your tax advisor before counting on these "pie-in-the-sky" deductions.

BEWARE

Find more detailed information on deductible travel expenses in Publication 463, Travel, Gift and Car Expenses.

Your Home As a Business Expense

Anyone who starts a business needs a place to work. You could work almost anywhere these days with all the technological advances and wireless internet in almost every bar, restaurant, café, hotel, and public place. However, you can also be strategic about where you choose to work, and you should definitely consider having a home office.

The benefit of the home office deduction is similar to needing a computer for your business; you can convert what would otherwise be a personal expenditure into a deductible business expenditure. You need a place to live and whether you rent or you own, you're incurring costs. Typically, most of these costs are not deductible—with the exception of mortgage interest expense and real estate taxes, and even those are subject to multiple limitations that take away the advantage of the deduction.

The home office deduction puts those costs and the other costs of maintaining a home into a completely different category of the tax code, which typically makes them more beneficial to you.

According to IRS Topic 509, the home office deduction is available to the following:

1. *Those that use a portion of their home exclusively on a regular basis as their principal place of business for their trade or business.*

2. *Those that use a portion of their home exclusively on a regular basis as a place to meet and deal with their patients, clients, or customers.*

3. *Those that use a separate structure, not attached to their home, which is used exclusively on a regular basis in connection with their trade or business.*

4. *Those that use a portion of their home on a regular basis for storage of inventory or product samples used in their trade or business of selling products at retail or wholesale.**

5. Those that rent out a portion of their home.

6. Those that regularly use a portion of their home as a day care facility.*

*You should note that the word "exclusive" was intentionally NOT included in numbers 4 or 6 above, as these do not require exclusive use. They do require "regular" use, though.

STRATEGY TIP

If you're an employee working remotely from home, you generally cannot take the home office deduction. However, there is an exception if you're working from home for the convenience of your employer, such as when your employer does not have physical office space. However, this deduction was put on hold until tax year 2026 as a result of the temporary elimination of employee business expenses.

Stocking Up on inventory

I had a client with a wholesale health company who created vitamins and sold them to local health and fitness stores. The cost of acquiring his inventory was lower per unit when he bought more, so he needed a significant amount of storage for his product. With the help of his tax advisor, my client decided it would be more efficient to use his home as a place to store inventory, allowing him to take the home office deduction, rather than adding additional business costs to rent or buy a storage facility.

This decision was efficient for two reasons. The first is obvious: Not having to rent a storage facility reduced the expenses incurred to run his business, which in turn increased the bottom line. The second is that he was now able to deduct the costs associated with that portion of his home against his income, which he otherwise would not have been able to do. This decision saved him additional expenses and dropped his tax bill by a more than an insignificant amount.

My client was able to avoid the exclusive use requirement, meaning he could use the same room where he stored inventory for other purposes throughout the year and still receive the deduction. This exception only applies for storage of inventory and not the other tasks you may perform for your business. Keep this in mind if your business requires inventory.

....

DEDUCING YOUR DEDUCTION

Those who qualify for the home office deduction can deduct the business portion of real estate taxes, mortgage interest, rent, casualty losses, utilities, insurance, depreciation, maintenance, and repairs. The question then becomes: "What is the business portion of these expenses?" There are two methods for determining the business portion of your home expenses that are deductible.

IN CASE OF AUDIT

There have been many taxpayers before you who attempted to take advantage of the home office deduction. The IRS will focus in on the exclusive use requirement and whether your home office is your main place of business. Organize your home office so it supports the determination you've made. Don't have your children's PlayStation hooked up to a TV in your home office.

The first method is called the "simplified option." We'll refer to this as the "lazy man's option." It will still produce positive results, but many times they won't be as beneficial as the next option we will discuss. The lazy man's method allows you to deduct $5 per square foot up to a maximum of 300 square feet. You can only use the square footage of your home that is used by the business, and which meets the requirements mentioned previously. This maxes out the deduction at $1,500 per year. A single taxpayer in the 22 percent tax bracket could save $330 in income tax. Additionally, business income is subject to self-employment taxes at a rate of 15.3 percent, so the deduction saves another $230 for a total of $560 of tax savings. That's nothing to sneeze at, but we can do better.

The second—more involved—method is referred to as the "regular option." This method requires more than one step. You must first determine the square footage of your home that is used by the business, and which meets the requirements mentioned previously relative to the total square footage of your home. This gives you the business use percentage of your home. Simply figuring the square footage of the portion used by your business means you are not limited to 300 square feet as you would be under the lazy man's method.

TAX TENET #14
Know your options.

The next step in determining your deduction is figuring out where your home expenses fit. Figure 8.2 details the different categories.

Figure 8.2. Home office business expenses fit into three categories

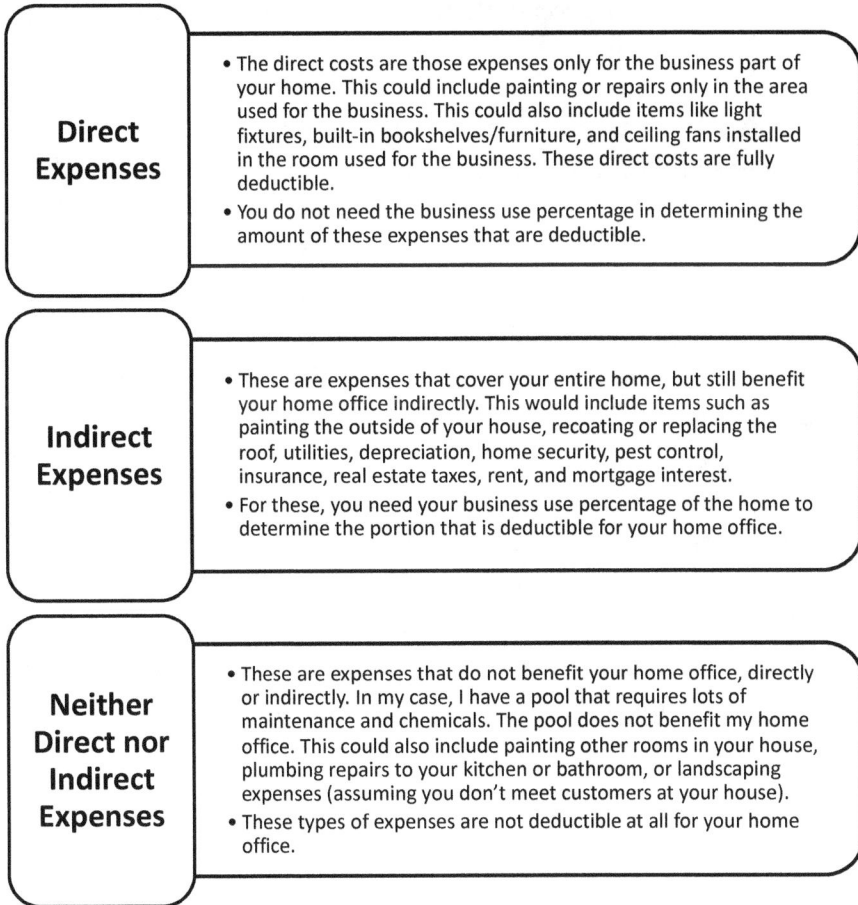

Direct Expenses	• The direct costs are those expenses only for the business part of your home. This could include painting or repairs only in the area used for the business. This could also include items like light fixtures, built-in bookshelves/furniture, and ceiling fans installed in the room used for the business. These direct costs are fully deductible. • You do not need the business use percentage in determining the amount of these expenses that are deductible.
Indirect Expenses	• These are expenses that cover your entire home, but still benefit your home office indirectly. This would include items such as painting the outside of your house, recoating or replacing the roof, utilities, depreciation, home security, pest control, insurance, real estate taxes, rent, and mortgage interest. • For these, you need your business use percentage of the home to determine the portion that is deductible for your home office.
Neither Direct nor Indirect Expenses	• These are expenses that do not benefit your home office, directly or indirectly. In my case, I have a pool that requires lots of maintenance and chemicals. The pool does not benefit my home office. This could also include painting other rooms in your house, plumbing repairs to your kitchen or bathroom, or landscaping expenses (assuming you don't meet customers at your house). • These types of expenses are not deductible at all for your home office.

BEWARE

Deductions for depreciation on your home office will require you to "recapture" those deductions at a maximum rate of 25 percent should you sell your home later. This portion of your home won't be available for the home sale exclusion described in Chapter 10.

BEWARE

You can find more detailed information on the home office deduction in Publication 587, Business Use of Your Home.

There's a lot to unpack here so let's do a quick example to show how powerful this deduction can be. Karen has a home office which she uses exclusively for business. The home office portion of her home is 300 square feet, and the total area of her home is 1,500 square feet. The home office represents 20 percent of her total home square footage (300 divided by 1,500). This is the business use percentage.

Using these amounts, Table 8.1 shows the various expenses that may be associated with Karen's home and how her deduction would be derived. Making some assumptions on the applicable tax rates, this table shows the approximate tax savings for each deduction. You can use this table to estimate your potential home office deduction by substituting your expenses and your tax rates.

According to Table 8.1, Karen's home office deduction puts an extra $5,570.90 in her pocket as shown by the "Total tax savings" line at the bottom. Now that's a nice tax benefit.

Table 8.1. Calculating the home office deduction and tax savings

Expense	Amount	Direct or Indirect	Business Percentage	Deduction	Tax Rate*	Tax Savings
Real estate taxes	$6,000	Indirect	20%	$1,200	49.30 %	$591.60
Mortgage interest	$15,000	Indirect	20%	$3,000	49.30 %	$1,479.00
Homeowner's insurance	$1,500	Indirect	20%	$300	49.30 %	$147.90
Utilities	$6,000	Indirect	20%	$1,200	49.30 %	$591.60
General repairs	$1,000	Indirect	20%	$200	49.30 %	$98.60
Office painting	$800	Direct	100%	$800	49.30 %	$394.40
Office furniture	$1,600	Direct	100%	$1,600	49.30 %	$788.80
Depreciation	$15,000	Indirect	20%	$3,000	49.30 %	$1,479.00
Total tax savings						$5,570.90

*Tax Rate: Assumes 24 percent federal income tax rate, plus 10 percent state income rate, plus 15.3 percent self-employment tax

This doesn't even include the potential for additional automobile deductions if she visits off-site business locations. Let's take a look at how automobile deductions can provide additional tax savings.

> ## BEWARE
> *The home office deduction is one of the only business deductions that is limited to the net income of your business. If Karen has $30,000 of gross business income and $26,000 of business expense, this leaves a $4,000 net profit before considering her home office deductions. If her home office deduction is $5,570, then only $4,000 would be deductible in the current year. But Karen can carry over the excess amount to future years to offset business income when she has enough net profit.*

Automobile Deductions

The automobile deduction allows you to write off all or a portion of your car-related expenses when used as part of a business. This deduction isn't allowed for employees even though they may use their vehicle in the course of their employment. The government recognizes that many businesses will put additional wear and tear on their vehicles when using them in their businesses and therefore provides tax incentives to reduce this burden.

This deduction is great because you probably already have a vehicle that you use and for which you are incurring loan or lease payments, maintenance, insurance, and other expenses. Many of these expenses will be the same regardless of whether you use the vehicle in a business or not. By incorporating the vehicle in your business, these expenses become deductible to you. You will of course likely incur additional gas or electric vehicle charges, but many times your tax savings will more than offset these costs.

I have always been a big fan of camping and driving on dirt roads, so I wanted a vehicle that could handle a lot of off-road driving and had the storage for gear. At the time I was looking to upgrade my vehicle, I had two main active businesses: accounting and real estate. As a CPA, I needed a vehicle I could use to meet clients, travel to business conferences, and visit our office outside of Tucson. For my real estate business, I needed to be able to haul tools and other items. The perfect mix for all my needs was a four-wheel drive pickup.

I needed the pickup to haul gear for my real estate business, a relatively fuel-efficient engine to meet clients, and a four-wheel drive for various towing and other scenarios related to my real estate business. I wouldn't be able to deduct the entire cost of the vehicle since there would be some personal use, but having a business use for the vehicle allowed me to essentially subsidize the cost of my off-roading hobby.

ACTUAL METHOD

There are two methods you can use when calculating your automobile deduction: the actual method and the standard mileage method. The cost of your vehicle plays a major role in determining which method is better.

The lower the cost of the vehicle, the better the mileage deduction becomes. Generally, for a vehicle that costs $30,000 or less, the mileage deduction will yield a higher tax savings. This can vary depending on the type of vehicle purchased and business and non-business miles driven.

The actual method involves figuring all your expenses related to the vehicle and taking a deduction equal to your business use percentage of those expenses. You can include the following expenses for the actual method:

- Interest expense (if owned)
- Lease payments (if leased)
- Gas and oil
- Repairs and maintenance
- Cleaning

- **Depreciation (if owned)**

- **Registration and licenses**

- **Insurance**

The most complex part of figuring your actual expenses is the depreciation deduction. There are a lot of nuances with vehicle depreciation depending on the cost of the vehicle, the type of vehicle, and the business use percentage. Don't try figuring out all of this on your own; that's what your CPA is for. But I will give you the general guidelines to get you started.

First you need to determine whether your business use percentage is above or below 50 percent. If your business use is 50 percent or more, you can use the **modified accelerated cost recovery system (MACRS).** This method allows you to take more deductions in the earlier years and fewer in the later years. In other words, you can front-load your deductions to receive the time value of money. If your business use is less than 50 percent, you must use the straight-line (SL) recovery method. As you might guess, this is simply the depreciation deductions spread out evenly. Table 8.2 indicates the percentage that is depreciated based on each of these methods.

Table 8.2. Depreciation deduction variables

Tax Year	MACRS	SL
1	20 percent	10 percent
2	32 percent	20 percent
3	19.20 percent	20 percent
4	11.52 percent	20 percent
5	11.52 percent	20 percent
6	5.76 percent	10 percent

BEWARE

*The **depreciable basis** of your vehicle when **placed in service** for your business is the lower of the purchase price or the fair market value. This applies when converting a vehicle that was previously used solely for personal use into business use. You can easily figure the fair market value by using online resources, such as the Blue Book.*

Notice under both methods that the percentage depreciated in the first year is less than the second year. This is because the IRS assumes the vehicle is placed in service on July 1, resulting in a half year of depreciation in the first year. Therefore, you're no better off rushing to purchase a vehicle in January than you are waiting to purchase that vehicle later in the year.

BEWARE

Although the IRS generally assumes a vehicle was purchased halfway through the year regardless of the actual purchase date, there is an exception. If you purchase the vehicle in the last quarter of the year, the IRS could force you to place the vehicle in service halfway through that last quarter, on November 1.

The last piece to the puzzle in figuring your depreciation deduction is the luxury automobile limits, which was enacted because taxpayers were purchasing more expensive vehicles that were not ordinary or necessary for their business. The expensive vehicles were purchased to increase their write-off even though the vehicle type was more of a personal desire than a business need. The limits mostly apply to passenger automobiles—defined as any four-wheeled vehicle that is made primarily for use on public streets and rated at an unloaded gross vehicle weight (GVW) of 6,000 pounds. The limit also applies to trucks or vans (as classified by the manufacturer) with a loaded GVW of 6,000 pounds or less. You'll want to check with your CPA for the maximum deduction in each year if these apply to you.

STRATEGY TIP

If the luxury automobile limits don't apply, you may be able to write off 100 percent of your vehicle costs, assuming 100 percent business use in the year of purchase. This is either through bonus depreciation or Section 179. For a truck, you'll likely want to make sure the bed length is six feet or more to maximize the deduction. Send a copy of the window sticker of the vehicle you're looking to purchase to your CPA to confirm your tax savings.

Let's look at an example of how the actual method works in practice. Let's assume you purchase a vehicle that is not subject to the luxury automobile limits for $60,000. Table 8.3 shows an example where accelerated depreciation can be used and one where straight line must be used.

Table 8.3. Two methods of depreciation

	Accelerated Depreciation	Straight-line Depreciation
Business miles	18,000	9,000
Total miles	20,000	20,000
Business use percentage	**90 percent**	**45 percent**
Operating expenses		
Gas and oil	$4,500	$4,500
Repairs and maintenance	$800	$800
Cleaning	$400	$400
Registration and licenses	$900	$900
Insurance	$1,200	$1,200
Interest expense	$900	$900
Total expenses before depreciation	**$8,700**	**$8,700**
Business use percentage	90 percent	45 percent
Deductible business portion expenses	**$7,830**	**$3,915**
Depreciation*	$54,000	$2,700
Total automobile deduction year 1	**$61,830**	**$6,615**

*Depreciation for the accelerated method is figured assuming 100 percent can be expensed in the first year multiplied by the business use percentage of 90 percent ($60,000 × 90 percent). Depending on the vehicle and the year in service, 100% depreciation may not be available. Depreciation for the straight-line method is figured by multiplying the business use percentage by the cost of the vehicle and then multiplying that by the 10 percent allowed in the first year ($60,000 × 45 percent × 10 percent).

I know, that was probably more math than you want to do—or even see. After all, you're probably not a CPA and have no desire to be. Let your accountant do the math for you, but make sure you keep all your receipts and records so you don't lose out on the deductions. As you can see from the table, the tax savings can be quite nice.

STANDARD MILEAGE RATE

Now let's talk about the second method for deducting automobile expenses, the standard mileage rate. This is a much easier math problem so hopefully I won't lose anyone here. Under this method, instead of figuring all your actual expenses and using the business use percentage, you simply multiply the standard mile rate determined by the IRS by your total **business miles** for the year.

For 2024, the IRS allows a standard business rate of 67 cents per mile. This amount is adjusted each year so make sure to check for updates. Here's how it works:

18,000 business miles × 67 cents = $12,060

Come on, I know you can do that math! Regardless, your job is simply to track your business mileage and let your CPA do the rest.

STRATEGY TIP

You can easily switch from using the standard mileage method to the actual expense method, but the IRS makes it hard to switch the other way around.

BUSINESS MILES

I keep mentioning "business miles," so I hope you're wondering what constitutes a business mile. I mean, that's an important part of the deduction after all. The rules on business mileage can get quite confusing.

The first step in understanding the idea of a "business mile" is to understand the difference between a temporary work location and a regular work location. A temporary work location is one you reasonably expect to last for less than one year. For example, if you're a contractor visiting a building site that you expect will be completed in less than a year, this would be a temporary work location. A regular work location is one you reasonably expect to remain in for more than one year. This is usually your main office, but it could also be other regular business locations like a bank or post office that you expect to use for more than a year.

The drive from your home (assuming it's not a home office) to your regular place of work is not considered business mileage. These are nondeductible commuting miles. However, going from your regular place of work to another regular place of work or to a temporary work location would be deductible.

All miles after stopping at a temporary work location or when driving between one regular work location to another work location are business miles. Therefore, if you stop at the bank for business and then head to your office, the mileage from the bank to your office would be business miles, but if you go straight from your home to the office, those miles would be nondeductible commuting miles.

STRATEGY TIP

Plan to drive to temporary work locations on your way to or from work to maximize your business miles and therefore your tax savings.

You can also consider all miles driven from your home to a temporary business location as business miles as long as you have a regular place of business or the temporary work location is outside your metropolitan area. For example, my main office as a CPA is in Tucson, Arizona. My commute from my home to the office is not considered business mileage. However, I have clients in Phoenix, Arizona, where I work occasionally. If I drive from my home to Phoenix to visit a client, all of those miles are business miles since it's a temporary work location. Table 8.4 defines the various locations used to determine business mileage, and Table 8.5 illustrates how the business mileage concept works.

Table 8.4. Definitions of locations to determine business mileage

Home	This is the place you reside.
Regular or main job	This is your principal place of business.
Second job	This applies when you regularly work two or more places in one day. This can be for the same job or a different job.
Temporary work location	This is a work location that is expected to last and does last one year or less.

Table 8.5. Guide for determining business mileage

Home to temporary work location	Only deductible if temporary work location is outside your metropolitan area or you have a regular or main job at another location
Temporary work location to home	Only deductible if temporary work location is outside your metropolitan area or you have a regular or main job at another location
Temporary work location to regular or main job	Deductible
Regular or main job to temporary work location	Deductible
Temporary work location to second job	Deductible
Second job to temporary work location	Deductible
Regular or main job to second job	Deductible
Second job to regular or main job	Deductible
Home to regular or main job	Nondeductible
Regular or main job to home	Nondeductible
Home to second job	Nondeductible
Second job to home	Nondeductible

STRATEGY TIP

Combining the home office and business mileage deductions is a way to kill two birds with one stone. If you have a home office, you can count every mile you drive every time you leave your house for a business purpose. You not only receive a deduction for the otherwise personal expenses of maintaining your home, but you also increase your eligible auto expenses!

PLAN AHEAD

While the business mileage rules seem somewhat intuitive when reading about them, frankly, there is a lot to keep straight. In fact, I bet most people taking the vehicle business expense deduction don't understand these rules. The best way to keep this straight is to think ahead about all your temporary and regular places of business. Figure out at the beginning of the year which trips would be business mileage and map out the deductible miles.

Once you do this, you will have to think much less about which miles are eligible on a day-to-day basis. There are even phone apps to help you keep track. You can designate temporary work locations, regular work locations, and your home, and the app will figure out the business miles for you. You want to automate this process as much as possible. After all, you have a business to run!

STRATEGY TIP

Employees are not able to deduct business mileage for any trips. This deduction was eliminated starting in 2018 with the Tax Cuts and Jobs Act. If you're an employee, check to see if your employer will reimburse for vehicle expenses, in which case the employer receives the deductions. But 100 percent reimbursement is better than a tax deduction anyway.

You should know that automobile expenses are one of the most audited items. To make sure you don't lose out on this valuable deduction, keep records of the following:

- Cost of the vehicle, including improvements
- Receipts and/or cancelled checks for all expenses
- The date you started using the vehicle for business
- The miles for each business use and total miles for the year
- The date of the business use
- The business destination
- The business purpose for the expense or business mileage

IN CASE OF AUDIT

I always recommend keeping a log of your business miles throughout the year. This is what the IRS agent will ask for if they decide to audit you. These days it's a lot easier because dozens of mobile phone apps can help you keep track. It is possible to prove your business purpose based on other evidence, but the auditor will be much more critical of your mileage if it's not kept in real time. Your best bet is to keep a regular log with the required documentation.

All this talk about business mileage is making me hungry! Let's move on to discuss the ways to maximize deductions for meals.

Meals

I'm a big foodie and I love trying new places to eat. When I can combine that love with some tax deductions to help subsidize my addiction, I've found heaven. Even if you're not a foodie, the ability to deduct meals that you must eat anyway can make a nice difference in your tax burden.

It used to be that meals and entertainment were somewhat synonymous with each other. You were allowed a deduction for entertainment before tax year 2018. However, this was changed with the Tax Cuts and Jobs Act. Now, entertainment is no longer deductible, but meals remain partially deductible.

STRATEGY TIP

Meals remain deductible as long as the expense is not lavish or extravagant under the circumstances and the taxpayer (or an employee) is present.

Generally, the IRS allows you to deduct only 50 percent of the cost of meals. However, there are some instances where this limitation does not apply and the entire cost of the meal is deductible. Table 8.6 can help you determine whether a meal is deductible and by what amount.

Table 8.6. Meal deductions

Business Meal Type	Deduction Amount
Meals when taxpayer or employee/contractor is not present	0 percent
Business meals with clients	50 percent
Business meals with work colleagues (employees, independent contractors, etc.)	50 percent
Meals while traveling for work	50 percent
Meals while attending work seminar, convention, or similar	50 percent
Dinner for employees working late at the office or meals for weekends	50 percent
Snacks for the office (coffee, donuts, soft drinks)	50 percent
Food for company social gatherings	100 percent
Food and beverages for the public (typically advertising events)	100 percent
Food as cost of goods sold (restaurants)	100 percent

BEWARE

Meals will often be included with entertainment expenses. For example, a box or seat at a sporting event may include meals. Only meals that are itemized on the receipt will be deductible. Make sure to itemize the meals separately to deduct them.

TALK SHOP OVER YOUR FOOD

You need to make sure business is discussed before, during, or after a business meal to qualify for a deduction. You can't simply take an employee to lunch and just talk about your kids and expect the meal to be deductible. Make sure you have a business purpose.

The surrounding environment is critical for the deductibility of meals. If it's not reasonable for business to be discussed in a specific location or that location is not conducive to a business discussion, the IRS will disallow the expense. For example, purchasing a meal at a theater or in a nightclub would indicate a location that does not allow for business conversation.

STRATEGY TIP

Make sure you keep separate accounts in your accounting system for the different meals. You'll want to separate them between nondeductible, 50 percent deductible, and 100 percent deductible. This can be a headache to determine if you wait till the end of the year, so make sure you track this throughout the year.

SCHEDULE SEMINARS AND PARTIES

Using seminars is a great way to create 100 percent deductible meals for you and your clients, vendors, and other business associates. My firm often holds real estate tax seminars and sends invitations to our clients and prospective clients. We give a tax update and sometimes invite someone in the real estate industry to give a presentation.

To enhance networking, we provide appetizers and drinks before and after the presentations. All of the food and beverages for these events are fully deductible since it is provided for the public. Also deductible would be food that real estate agents provide at open houses.

You can also take advantage of the meal deductions by holding business parties at your home. You'll need to establish a clear business purpose for the party. For example, inviting clients over to network or promote a new service or product—theirs or yours—will establish a business purpose.

Document who was there, why they were invited, and the business purpose of the gathering. Keep separate receipts for the meals and beverages provided outside of your regular household groceries. Business meals at your home are usually eligible for only a 50 percent deduction, but structuring the gathering as a seminar will make them 100 percent deductible since the meals will be provided for the public. You can also deduct 100 percent of the meals provided at your home for employee social gatherings.

Substantiate each business meal and its purpose. Most record-keeping requirements can be satisfied with a receipt. Note on the receipt or in your accounting records the business purpose of the meal and who was present at the meal. Table 8.7 shows the details you need to supply to document your meal expenses.

Table 8.7. Meal expenses documentation

Substantiation Requirements	
1.	Amount of the expense
2.	Date of the expense
3.	Location of the expense
4.	Business purpose of the meal
5.	Who was present at the meal

IN CASE OF AUDIT

Similar to travel expenses, you don't actually need to keep receipts for expenses under $75. However, I highly encourage you to keep those receipts anyway. Show the IRS that you are operating a real business so they take you seriously.

The rules for business meals are obviously quite nuanced, and they also change quite frequently. I recommend categorizing each of your potential meals at the beginning of the year using the categories seen in Table 8.6. This will make it easier to record them in the correct category for your CPA at the end of the year. It's also a good idea to check with your CPA at the beginning of each year to make sure there are no changes to the rules regarding meal deductions.

IN CASE OF AUDIT

I have seen a lot of interesting ideas for deducting meals on social media lately. Be careful where you get your tax advice. Mixing business with your friends for deductions or going to meals frequently (daily or weekly) with the same people under the guise of business—even if you have a true business relationship—can be a fast track to an IRS audit.

TAX TENET #15

Creative advice isn't always good advice.

Chapter Summary

✓ **Good tax planning can help you convert** nondeductible personal expenses into deductible business expenses.

✓ Proper substantiation of business purpose and expenses is critical in case of an audit.

✓ The primary purpose for deductible travel expenses must be related to your business.

✓ Combining the home office deduction with automobile mileage can multiply your tax savings.

✓ Make sure to separate out meals into nondeductible, 50 percent deductible, and 100 percent deductible expenses.

✓ Be careful where you get tax advice.

9

MEET DEPRECIATION, YOUR NEW BEST FRIEND

When I was growing up, I often heard that a new car would lose half its value as soon as I drove it off the lot. That warning about a new car purchase was a way of explaining the concept of depreciation or a **depreciating asset.**

The federal tax code recognizes that not all assets have an indefinite life, while it also recognizes that many assets you use for your business last longer than one year. You need to understand this concept when you are making large purchases that you expect will lower your tax bill. If your tax-deductible asset is expected to last for more than a year, you cannot take a deduction for the full cost of the purchase in the year you acquired it. Instead, the tax code tells you how long an asset is expected to last and allows you to take partial deductions over that specified time period, which is referred to as the **useful life** of an asset.

Different depreciation methods are available depending on the specific asset and some choices you make. The two most common methods these days are **straight-line depreciation** and **modified accelerated cost recovery system (MARCS).**

> ⚠️ **BEWARE**
>
> *Depreciation is only available for business use assets. You cannot take depreciation deductions for personal-use assets.*

Straight-line depreciation is fairly straightforward. No pun intended. Divide the cost of the asset by its useful life in years or months to find the amount you can deduct during a specified time period. For example, if you purchase an asset for $100,000 and it is deemed to have a useful life of five years, you would divide $100,000 by five to arrive at an annual depreciation amount of $20,000.

The accelerated recovery system front-loads the process so that you receive larger deductions in the early years of the asset's expected useful life and smaller ones in the latter years. In most cases, this is the preferred depreciation method because you will realize the benefits of the depreciation deductions sooner.

However, the accelerated recovery method is not available for all asset types, and there are also different rates of acceleration depending on the specific asset. For example, automobiles, furniture, and equipment will have a faster rate of depreciation than fences, parking lots, and outside lighting even though all of these are eligible for accelerated depreciation.

You may have an opinion on how long you think your purchase will last. The tax code does not care about your opinion. The IRS assigns each asset to a category that determines its useful life and available depreciation method(s). Sometimes the IRS assigned life and method are accurate and correspond with real-life depreciation, but sometimes the paper values seem far from real life. Heck, I'm still driving a 1972 Toyota Land Cruiser. According to the tax code, this vehicle would have been worthless after five years. That was almost fifty years ago!

That's an extreme example, but it shows how tax code values can be very far from real-life values. This split can be common in real estate. Generally, the tax code says residential real estate loses all its value after twenty-seven years and six months and commercial real estate loses all its value after thirty-nine years. How many buildings do you drive by daily that are more than forty years old and selling for much more than they did when originally built?

The real estate depreciation standards are what can be called a "fake" deduction because the depreciation on paper does not necessarily correspond to a real-life **economic loss**. Normally, people don't like fake things, but fake deductions should be your favorite kind because the ability to take a tax deduction that doesn't correspond to any real economic loss is the best way to reduce your taxes. An example of this would be an asset that you purchase that has no actual value change or one that does not follow the IRS determined depreciation amount. If you purchase an asset for $10,000 and you have first-year depreciation of $2,000, but the asset could still be sold for $9,000, then you have a $1,000 actual or economic loss, and a $1,000 paper loss (the difference between the actual value loss and the allowed depreciation deduction).

TAX TENET #16
Depreciation can either work for you or against you, depending on the asset.

Table 9.1 describes the assigned depreciable life of the most common assets. It does not show all the potential assets that will fall into each class, but this should cover more than 90 percent of instances that you'll come across unless you're in a specialized industry. I've bolded the most common asset types and useful lives you will encounter.

Table 9.1. Assigned depreciable life of most common assets

Useful Life	Property
3 Years	Tractors (over the road use), race horses over 2 years old, any other horse over 12 years old
5 Years	**Automobiles, office equipment, appliances, carpets, furniture (used in residential rental real estate activity), machinery used in farming, breeding cattle, and dairy cattle**
7 Years	**Office furniture and fixtures, used agricultural machinery and equipment**
10 Years	Vessels, barges, tugs, any tree or vine bearing fruits or nuts, any single-purpose agricultural or horticultural structure
15 Years	**Certain improvements made directly to land or on it (land improvements), including fences, parking lots, roads, sidewalks, bridges, etc.**
20 Years	Farm buildings
25 Years	Water utility property
27.5 Years	**Residential real property**
39 Years	**Nonresidential real property**

BEWARE

You'll notice that land is not found in Table 9.1. This is because the tax code does not allow you to depreciate land.

Depreciation Exceptions—
There Are Always Exceptions

There are a slew of exceptions when it comes to depreciation. Although the tax code generally requires you to receive deductions for large purchases over a specified period, there are two main code sections that may allow you to receive all—or at least most—of the tax benefits in the first year. Those two sections are bonus depreciation and Section 179.

IN CASE OF AUDIT

There are some assets that may have a personal use component, like automobiles. Make sure to document the business use to secure your depreciation deductions.

Bonus Depreciation

Bonus depreciation has been around for a couple of decades. It allows you to expense a certain percentage of an asset in the first year, with the remaining percentage depreciated over the specified time period for that asset. Qualifying assets placed in service between September 27, 2017, and January 1, 2023, are eligible for 100 percent bonus depreciation. Qualifying assets placed in service during 2023 are eligible for 80 percent bonus depreciation.

For tax year 2024, the bonus depreciation percentage is 60 percent. Each year thereafter, the bonus depreciation amount is reduced by 20 percent. Table 9.2 can serve as a quick reference to the bonus depreciation rate in each year.

Table 9.2. Bonus depreciation rates

Tax Year Placed in Service	Special Bonus Depreciation Rate
2022	100 %
2023	80 %
2024	60 %
2025	40 %
2026	20 %
After 2026	0 %

Not all property is eligible for bonus depreciation, but generally any tangible property with a useful life of twenty years or less will be eligible. You can reference the useful life table in Table 9.1 to see which assets qualify. Most equipment, furniture, electronics, automobiles, and other personal property (movable) will qualify for bonus depreciation. Additionally, land improvements such as parking lots, roads, sidewalks, and fences will qualify.

BEWARE

Make sure to review the luxury auto limits in Chapter 8 for potential limitations on bonus depreciation and Section 179 for automobiles.

Another common item that qualifies for bonus depreciation is referred to as **qualified improvement property**, which is generally property that improves the interior of nonresidential real estate. It must be placed in service after the building being improved was first placed in service. However, these improvements are not included:

- Enlargement of the building
- Elevators or escalators
- Internal structural framework of the building

STRATEGY TIP

One major benefit of bonus depreciation is it can create a loss for your business, so you can use the depreciation to offset your other income. Section 179, on the other hand, is limited to the amount of income for the business prior to taking the Section 179 deduction along with other limitations.

SECTION 179

The Section 179 expense has been part of the tax code for much longer than bonus depreciation, well over sixty years, actually. It provides another way to take depreciation deductions faster.

Section 179 allows you to fully deduct up to $1,220,000 of qualifying assets for 2024. However, if the total amount of qualifying property exceeds $3,050,000 in any given year, you must reduce the $1,220,000 dollar limit by the amount that your qualifying assets exceed this amount. Once you place $4,270,000 of assets in service in a single year, you can no longer take any Section 179 expense. These dollar limits are subject to change, so you'll want to check them each year.

STRATEGY TIP

When possible, take advantage of bonus depreciation before Section 179. There are many more limits associated with Section 179 expense.

For the most part, the same assets that qualify for bonus depreciation will be qualified for Section 179 expense. This includes most personal property and qualified improvement property, as described previously.

STRATEGY TIP

Land improvements do not qualify for Section 179. You'll want to use bonus depreciation for these assets.

One lesser-known benefit of Section 179 is that the following items, which are not typically eligible for Bonus Depreciation, are eligible for Section 179:

- **Roofs**

- **Heating, ventilation, and air-conditioning**

- **Fire protection and alarm systems**

- **Security systems**

With bonus depreciation and Section 179 rules in place, most assets are eligible to be expensed in the first year even when they have a longer useful life. This method of lowering taxes is the government's way of incentivizing businesses to spend and reinvest—to create more value for society. The percentages and dollar amounts for both Bonus Depreciation and Section 179 change frequently. You'll want to look for updates by visiting TaxStrategiesForEveryone.com.

You will notice two main asset classes don't qualify for these tax benefits: residential real property and nonresidential property. However, there are plenty of tax benefits for real estate. In fact, there are so many benefits that I've dedicated Chapter 10 to real estate.

STRATEGY TIP

There may be instances when you will not want to elect bonus depreciation or Section 179. One example of this would be when it would create a net operating loss on your personal income tax return. Net operating losses can only offset 80 percent of your taxable income in future years. You might be better off taking the deductions over time to avoid this limitation.

Depreciation Recapture

This chapter would not be complete without a short discussion on ***depreciation recapture.*** The cost basis you use to calculate your gain is reduced by depreciation deductions, which increases your gain when you sell. Most assets, including real estate and assets used in your business, will generate capital gains. Depreciation recapture results in paying a higher tax rate to the extent that you took depreciation deductions. However, the recaptured amount is limited to the amount of the gain. See Table 9.3 for an illustration of the process.

Table 9.3. Depreciation recapture

Depreciation Less Than Gain	
Sales Price	$100,000
Less: Original Cost	$50,000
Less: Depreciation	($10,000)
Adjusted Basis	$40,000
Gain	$60,000
Depreciation Recapture	$10,000
Capital Gain	$50,000

Depreciation Recapture Limited to Gain	
Sales Price	$45,000
Less: Original Cost	$50,000
Less: Depreciation	($10,000)
Adjusted Basis	$40,000
Gain	$5,000
Depreciation Recapture	$5,000
Capital Gain	$0

The rate of tax paid on depreciation recapture depends on the asset that is sold. Most personal property will have depreciation recapture applied at your ordinary income tax rates. Most real estate will have a maximum depreciation recapture rate of 25 percent.

Although you may have to pay tax on some depreciation deductions when you sell, it's still in your best interest to maximize these deductions. You'll receive the deduction saving taxes now, which puts money in your pocket that you can use immediately. Many times, especially with real estate, you will also pay a lower rate later after those deductions are recaptured.

Speaking of real estate, let's move on to Chapter 10 and my favorite topic.

IN CASE OF AUDIT

*Your CPA should prepare what's called a **depreciation schedule** to calculate and track your depreciation deductions over time. You'll want to make sure you have this as it will be necessary when you sell or otherwise dispose of an asset.*

....

Chapter Summary

✓ *Assets that are expected to last over one year must be depreciated rather than expensed.*

✓ *The IRS determines the useful life of an asset, which may not correspond to the true life of an asset.*

✓ *Bonus depreciation and Section 179 expense can allow you to write off most or all of an asset's cost even when its useful life is greater than a year.*

✓ *You will generally want to try to take bonus depreciation before Section 179 expense. However, this will change as the bonus depreciation percentage continues to decline.*

✓ *Depreciation deductions may need to be recaptured upon sale.*

✓ *Consider whether you should elect not to take bonus depreciation or Section 179 depending on your other income and deductions.*

10

IT'S TRUE: THE GOVERNMENT PRACTICALLY PAYS YOU TO INVEST IN REAL ESTATE

There is perhaps no area in the tax law as beneficial as the rules that deal with owning real estate. That's why I call real estate the wealthy person's treasure chest, at least when it comes to taxes. I'm sure you've seen and read debates about whether real estate owners pay less than their "fair" share of taxes.

Whatever side of the argument you fall on, there are undeniable truths. For one, real estate satisfies basic human need for shelter. We all need a place to live and call home. And also a place to work and grow food and make products and sell products. Residential and commercial real estate provide for those needs. That creates a value for society.

But actually owning and putting real estate to use has always been a capital-intensive endeavor, which means it also involves significant risk. It involves a risk of capital to build, buy, maintain, and utilize real estate. But if you do it well, you can create the kind of value the government rewards, which is why you will find so many tax advantages in this area. Remember our higher value/lower taxes concept?

TAX TENET #17

Real estate is one of the greatest tax shelters you can have.

Tax Benefits for Homeowners

Even if you don't want to invest in a real estate business, you should still consider the huge tax advantages you get from simply owning your home. When you rent, there is no benefit to you from a tax lens. You do not receive a deduction for the rent you pay or generate any type of tax-advantaged income. This contrasts with the substantial tax benefits of owning your own home.

Let's start with the low-hanging fruit. As discussed previously, you can receive a tax deduction for the mortgage interest paid on your own home and another tax deduction for real estate taxes paid. This is already more than you would receive as a renter. Therefore, the after-tax benefits of owning real estate must be considered with the after-tax benefits of renting.

HOME SALE EXCLUSION

According to recent statistics, Americans are expected to move 11.7 times in their lifetime—about every five years. I'm not sure about you, but I don't know anyone who enjoys the process of moving. Wouldn't it be great if there were a benefit involved to make the whole experience better? You might be surprised to learn that there is in fact a benefit, a huge benefit if you plan accordingly.

The IRS allows married taxpayers to exclude from their income up to $500,000 of appreciation on their principal residence when they sell it. Single taxpayers enjoy a very generous exclusion of up to $250,000. As with all tax benefits, there are, of course, requirements. You must own and live in a home for a time period equaling at least two years within the most recent five-year period. You can only take advantage of this exclusion at least two years apart from each use.

STRATEGY TIP

For most Americans, being able to exclude appreciation from the sale of their home every two years isn't an issue since most move on average every five years. If the average person moves 12 times in their lifetime and they are able to maximize the home sale exclusion each move, that would mean $3 million of tax-free income per individual!

A Home Is More Than a Place to Live

My client Larry operated a successful business and needed something to do with the earnings. He made the wise decision to purchase homes on a regular basis. He would live in the homes for at least two years, then upgrade to a larger and more expensive home. Each time he sold his home, he would enjoy the home sale exclusion for the appreciation. This allowed him to accumulate large amounts of tax-free income over many years. He ended up retiring in his forties without even needing to be a landlord.

Real Estate as a Business

Clearly the government incentivizes homeownership by giving perks to homeowners. Real estate as a business is like homeownership —on steroids. When I say "real estate as a business," I essentially mean owning real estate that is not your main or second home. In other words, real estate you do not personally use. This could mean a rental property, an investment property (held mainly for appreciation), or real estate used by your business.

Real estate used by your business could be the office building you purchased to house your dental practice, the retail corner spot where you opened your restaurant, or the warehouse used to manufacture or store your products. As a business owner, you can choose to rent or buy. Again, the tax code will favor those who own.

Real Estate Depreciates?

In Chapter 9, we talked about how depreciation generally works. However, the depreciation expense maximizes your deductions and wealth as it is applied to real estate more than it does with any other asset. Most assets you purchase in or for your business will lose value over time. Cars or specialized tools or equipment that you purchase for your business and depreciate on your taxes actually do lose value. There are few exceptions to this rule, so it makes logical sense that you will be able to take a deduction for this loss of value over time.

However, most real estate will actually appreciate over time. I'm not saying that all real estate always goes up in value. However, the majority of real estate assets will appreciate over a long enough period of time. Exceptions do not disprove the rule.

The wealth-building power of taking depreciation deductions against an appreciating asset cannot be undervalued. I know most people are not interested in math or finances and simply glaze over whenever someone mentions numbers. However, there is no better way to explain the incredible benefits of this concept without showing you some numbers. I'll keep it simple, but I want you to really study the examples in this chapter and accept that you need to know some numbers in this case. Remember, if you're not miserable, you're not learning.

RUN THE NUMBERS

When I was starting out as an investor in real estate, I put together a spreadsheet to calculate my *cash flow, taxable income,* and economic income from a potential real estate acquisition. Each of these numbers is important to understand when analyzing an investment and your after-tax rate of return.

Cash flow. The cash flow is probably the easiest to understand. This is simply going to be the difference between the cash in your bank account at the end of the year as compared to the cash in your bank account at the beginning of the year. If there's more cash in the bank at the end of the year than there was at the beginning then there is positive cash flow. There is negative cash flow when the opposite is true. See Table 10.1. Easy enough, right?

Table 10.1. Cash-flow statement

Date	Bank Account Balance
January 1	$4,500
December 31	$6,000
Annual cash flow:	
+$1,500	

IN CASE OF AUDIT

Make sure to have a separate bank account for each business. Run all your business expenses through that account and don't pay any personal expenses through it.

Taxable income. The taxable income is the amount your tax is based upon. Two items typically make your taxable income different from your cash flow: depreciation and principal payments on debt service. Depreciation causes a difference because it's a tax deduction that does not correspond to a cash outflow.

Most monthly debt payments will contain a portion that is a reduction of the debt (principal) and a portion that is interest expense (cost for using the debt). Principal payments on debt do not reduce your taxable income because this is simply the reduction of an asset (cash) with a corresponding reduction of a liability (debt). There is no income effect to a principal payment even though it reduces the cash available. See Table 10.2.

Table 10.2. Effects on taxable income

	Effects on	
	Cash Flow	**Taxable Income**
Depreciation	NA	($3,000)
Principal payment	($2,000)	NA
Interest payment	($2,500)	($2,500)
Net Effect	**($4,500)**	**($5,500)**

Economic income. Economic income is your taxable income after you have replaced the depreciation deduction with the actual change in value of the asset. If the asset appreciates, the negative depreciation becomes a positive number, increasing your economic income. You'll notice in Table 10.3 that the taxable income is the greatest negative. This is good because it means your tax savings will be greater.

You'll also notice that the economic income is the least negative. This reflects the difference between assets appreciating in reality while the IRS allows you to treat the asset as if it's depreciating. The effect on cash flow is in between both of these numbers.

Of course, it's possible that the numbers don't fall in this order, but Table 10.3 displays the optimal effect of a good investment.

Table 10.3. Key items affecting cash flow, taxable income, and economic income

	Effects on		
	Cash Flow	**Taxable Income**	**Economic Income**
Depreciation	NA	($3,000)	NA
Appreciation	NA	NA	$2,000
Principal payment	($2,000)	NA	NA
Interest payment	($2,500)	($2,500)	($2,500)
Net Effect	**($4,500)**	**($5,500)**	**($500)**

The cash flow, taxable income, and economic income are all negative at this point because we are only taking into account the differences between each. At this point, we have not included all the other income and expense items that will factor into these areas. So let's add the rest of the numbers into the analysis and examine them in Table 10.4 to see the potential difference between cash flow, taxable income, and economic income.

Table 10.4. Comparison of cash flow, taxable income, and economic income

	Effect On		
	Cash Flow	Taxable Income	Economic Income
Rental income	$17,000	$17,000	$17,000
Insurance	($1,000)	($1,000)	($1,000)
Property tax	($1,500)	($1,500)	($1,500)
Repairs	($800)	($800)	($800)
Property management	($1,700)	($1,700)	($1,700)
Depreciation	NA	($3,000)	NA
Appreciation	NA	NA	$2,000
Principal payment	($2,000)	NA	NA
Interest payment	($2,500)	($2,500)	($2,500)
Net Effect	**$7,500**	**$6,500**	**$11,500**

Look at the net effect numbers in Table 10.4. Remember, economic income represents the true increase to your wealth. Despite an $11,500 increase to your wealth, the IRS will only tax $6,500. That's $5,000 tax-free! If you ignore the appreciation available when considering economic income and compare your cash flow to taxable income, that's still $1,000 tax-free.

This is only the start. Once you take this simple concept of depreciation and layer on the other tax benefits you can claim with real estate, you'll be amazed at how much impact a reduction in taxes can make to your wealth.

Perform Cost Segregation Study

*You can greatly increase the tax benefits of depreciation by perform-ing a **cost segregation** study on real property. Rather than taking the IRS specified useful life of the real estate as a whole, break down the different components of the real estate into shorter useful lives.*

This allows you to take more of the depreciation deductions ear-lier on in the ownership of your property and can drive huge tax losses—which amounts to tax savings for you. All without affecting your cash flow.

If you own any real property, be sure to ask your CPA about this idea. This can be an absolute game changer.

Harness the Mighty Power of the 1031

We learned previously that when you sell something, you pay tax on the difference between the sales price and the **cost basis** of the asset. Many times, this will result in capital gain unless there is depreciation recapture. However, the government recognizes if you sell one piece of real estate and purchase another piece of real estate, you may not actually have the cash to pay the tax. Because investing in real estate is an action the government has determined is valuable to society, it wants to make it as economically feasible as possible to help you invest in real estate.

So, in comes the almighty *1031 exchange*—named after the Internal Revenue Code Section 1031. A 1031 is a tax-deferred exchange of real property for other real property.

Section 1031 says when you sell a real property asset and acquire another real property asset, you won't pay tax on that sale. However, this is a deferral of tax, not a permanent exclusion. You would pay tax on the sale and appreciation of the replacement real property when you sell the property acquired in the exchange. Assuming, of course, that you don't further defer the tax by performing another 1031 exchange. See Figure 10.1 for more 1031 requirements.

TAX TENET #18

A deferral of tax is usually better than paying the tax now. This puts the time value of money on your side.

Figure 10.1. Requirements to qualify for 1031 exchange

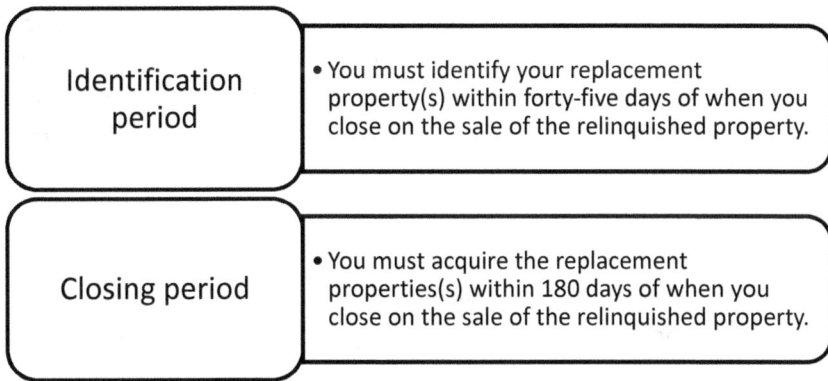

Identification period	• You must identify your replacement property(s) within forty-five days of when you close on the sale of the relinquished property.
Closing period	• You must acquire the replacement properties(s) within 180 days of when you close on the sale of the relinquished property.

A 1031 exchange is most useful when you would rather have a different property—not when you would like to increase your holdings by purchasing an additional property. If you want to keep your existing property and purchase another one, there are other tax-friendly strategies, such as the cash-out refinance we will discuss later in this chapter.

STRATEGY TIP

Equity is the value of the asset minus the debt. The return on equity is the cash flow divided by your equity. Therefore, your return on equity can change as the value of the asset changes. This is an important concept to recognize as you make investment decisions and can factor into why you would choose a 1031 exchange.

The 1031 identification rules are tricky, in addition to carrying a forty-five-day requirement. The IRS will only let you identify a certain number or value of properties. This is to prevent you from identifying multiple properties without really having a **replacement property** in mind, effectively circumventing the rules. Work with an exchange accommodator to make sure you don't run afoul of these rules.

> ### BEWARE
> *I want to drive this deep inside your brain: It's 180 days, not six months. You need to pay attention to that minor distinction. I've actually seen 1031s fail because someone was thinking in terms of months instead of days. Don't let this ruin your exchange.*

Also note that you can't take receipt of the proceeds from the sale of the **relinquished property.** You'll need an exchange intermediary (accommodator) to hold the proceeds in escrow while you wait to close on the replacement property. Legally speaking, the exchange intermediary is treated as the seller of the property and is the one who receives the proceeds from the sale and acquires the replacement property. This is to prevent you from receiving "boot" in the exchange.

Boot is when you take receipt of the proceeds in an exchange or when you receive an asset other than real estate in the exchange. For example, let's say you sold a property for $1 million but you bought replacement real estate worth only $800,000. This means you would receive $200,000 of proceeds that were not reinvested in real estate. This would be your boot and would result in recognizing some or all of the gain on the sale of your real estate.

STRATEGY TIP

You'll want to understand the difference between a **realized gain** *and a* **recognized gain.** *A realized gain may or may not be subject to tax. A recognized gain is subject to tax. In an exchange of property, you will have a realized gain on the sale of your property. However, if you properly execute a 1031 exchange, the gain will not be recognized.*

To prevent boot, make plans to cover your sales price and cover your debt. This means purchasing a replacement property with a cost equal to or greater than the sales price of your relinquished property. Make sure the debt you take on to purchase the replacement property is at least as much as the debt you had on your relinquished property at the time of sale.

IN CASE OF AUDIT

An exchange intermediary should supply you with a packet at the end of the exchange. This packet will contain the relevant items needed in the event of an audit, including the date the relinquished property was sold, the properties identified, the date of the identification, the date you acquired the replacement property, and the purchase and sales prices of the properties.

The real power of the 1031 exchange is you'll have more cash to acquire your replacement property rather than paying an extra bill to the government. It's obvious that a 1031 exchange can be a valuable tool for reducing your tax burden and therefore increasing your wealth. However, you must not forget that those tax savings are borrowed, since this is a deferral. But in Chapter 12, I'll show you an exception that can make those taxes go away forever.

> ⚠️ **BEWARE**
>
> *Prorations of property taxes, insurance, rents, and other items can cause boot to be received as these items are treated like cash in the exchange. Therefore, if you receive a net credit between the purchase and sale in an exchange of two properties from these items it's treated as if you received cash. Consult your CPA before closing to make sure this won't cause an issue in your exchange.*

Get the Preferential Treatment for Your Real Estate Sales

The sale of real estate is typically taxed at the preferential capital gains rate. Selling a property and recognizing a gain of $100,000 will often result in paying half the amount of taxes you would pay on $100,000 of ordinary income you earned as an employee or as a business owner or self-employed entrepreneur.

> ⚠️ **BEWARE**
>
> *Those who are considered to hold real estate as inventory will not receive the benefit of lower capital gains rates. This category would include real estate flippers and real estate developers who purchase or build the property with the intent to sell. Such transactions will result in ordinary income tax rates.*

Preferential tax rates will even apply when you consider depreciation recapture. As you hopefully remember, depreciation recapture is the income you are taxed on for taking depreciation deductions that did not actually correspond to the loss in value of an asset.

Let's say you took $40,000 in depreciation deductions on a property that was purchased for $500,000. The depreciation deductions are taken at an ordinary tax rate, meaning they offset your tax liability from other ordinary income items, like wages, salary, self-employment, and business income. This can result in a 37 percent tax savings when you're in the highest marginal rate. See Table 10.5 for an example of what happens when you sell that property for $560,000.

Table 10.5. How the sale of real estate is taxed

Purchase price	$500,000
(Less) depreciation	$40,000
Adjusted basis	$460,000
Sales price	$560,000
(Less) adjusted basis	$460,000
Gain	$100,000
Taxed as depreciation recapture (25 percent)	$40,000
Taxed as capital gain (20 percent)	$60,000

Your gain is $100,000 as a result of a reduced cost basis. Although you must recapture those depreciation deductions up to $40,000, the maximum rate you'll pay on that income is 25 percent. This is still much lower than the rate you received on those deductions! Additionally, the gain above the depreciation deductions will retain its capital gains status. Not many places in the tax code offer that kind of double benefit.

SOMETIMES YOU LOSE

Even when you do everything right, sometimes things don't go your way. Invest long enough in real estate, you may run into a situation where you have a loss. We already know you receive lower capital gains rates when you sell real estate at a profit. What happens when you have a loss?

Most assets that are capital gain property and result in preferential tax rates upon sale will also result in a capital loss. Remember, capital losses are limited to offsetting other capital gain income, or up to $3,000 dollars of your other types of income (for individual taxpayers). That would not be an ideal situation.

But the IRS allows the best of both worlds when it comes to real estate. When you sell real estate that is used in a trade or business—which generally applies to rental property—a resulting loss will be treated as an ordinary loss. This means there is no limit to the type of income and how much income this loss can offset, unlike a capital loss.

BEWARE

Property held as investment, meaning held mainly for appreciation, will not receive ordinary loss treatment. The most common example would be vacant land that was purchased as an investment but later sold at a loss. In this case, you would have a capital loss.

Deductions with OPM (Other People's Money)

It's a well-known fact that one of the biggest advantages of real estate is leverage. Most people mention this concept in terms of purchasing larger properties and maximizing a rate of return. Those are certainly advantages of leverage, but the benefits don't stop there. The tax code allows you to effectively "lose" other people's money and take deductions for it. Yes, that's right: You can take deductions against someone else's investment.

AN OPM EXTREME

I'm going to give you an extreme example of an OPM deduction. It's extreme but true. My second investment property purchase was a duplex back in 2013, and it was a difficult purchase, to say the least.

I spent months negotiating the purchase from a retired attorney, and it seemed like every week I found another problem with the property that I would need to solve. The seller had a loan on the property for about $110,000 at an 8 percent rate. By the time we were done negotiating, I had worked it out so the seller would receive no cash. Instead, she agreed that I would simply take over her existing loan at $110,000 to purchase the property.

Surprisingly, the bank agreed. I guess this was because interest rates were in the 4 percent range at the time, and it was happy to keep a loan at a higher interest rate.

The depreciation expense for my $110,000 property was about $3,200 a year after considering that only 80 percent of the value was depreciable. I couldn't depreciate 20 percent of the purchase that was attributed to the land value, but I was able to take this $3,200 deduction despite having no investment in the property because the tax code allows you to take rental real estate losses against most types of debt.

IN CASE OF AUDIT

You can use the county assessor's land value to document to the IRS the portion that is depreciable or not depreciable.

I don't think you need to be a tax nerd to get excited about that! I didn't have any cash outlay of my own and the depreciation deductions were a "fake" loss! This property was worth around $400,000 in 2022 and I could still take depreciation deductions.

I know my example is unique because it involves a zero-down purchase. However, you can find many ways to benefit from taking deductions against OPM. I know because I see it happen all the time for my clients.

You can get a similar benefit from owning a property long enough that the depreciation deductions outweigh your cash investment, although this may take many years. You can get this result faster by performing the cost segregation study, which I mentioned earlier in the chapter, thereby accelerating the depreciation deductions.

One of my favorite ways to get this result is the cash-out refinance, which is coming up next.

....

Debt Awareness

Be aware that the type of debt does matter when you are looking at deductions. There are generally three types of debt for tax purposes.

1. *Nonrecourse debt means it is not secured by the property and you have not guaranteed the debt (not personally responsible).*

2. *Qualified nonrecourse debt is the same as nonrecourse except that it's secured by the real estate. This is a special category of debt in the tax code to allow taxpayers to do exactly what I did with my duplex in 2013.*

3. *Recourse debt means you have guaranteed or are personally liable for the debt, regardless of whether it's secured by real property or not.*

You can take depreciation deductions against both recourse and qualified nonrecourse debt. You cannot take depreciation deductions against nonrecourse debt.

....

Cash-out Tax-Free

Another great tax benefit way to owning real estate can be found in a cash-out refinance. I'll explain this benefit by continuing to tell you about my 2013 duplex purchase. After I purchased the duplex by taking over the loan for $110,000, I slowly made various improvements over the years with the rental income I received. I remodeled the kitchens, installed new tile and carpet, and hung nicer doors.

These improvements—along with the natural rent growth and appreciation of real estate—meant my equity in the investment grew significantly. By the time 2021 arrived, the value of the property had tripled. Additionally, I could get a loan for the property at less than 4 percent interest rate!

In 2021, I decided it was the optimal time to refinance at a higher loan amount to get some cash out of the property. By this time, my loan had been paid down to about $100,000, but I decided to increase my loan to $200,000, which meant I would cash out of the property with $100,000 from a refinance. This was easily possible because of the equity that had been built in the property.

Sometime around April 2021, $100,000 hit my bank account. I could do anything I wanted with the cash. Do you know what the best part was? I didn't have to pay any tax on the cash I received! The IRS doesn't tax cash-out refinances. This is because you are still on the hook for paying that money back at some point.

BEWARE

The interest expense on the additional debt from a cash-out refinance may or may not be deductible. The IRS requires you to trace the proceeds of the cash-out to determine whether it is deductible. The details of this requirement are beyond the scope of this book so make sure to consult with your tax advisor.

These tax advantages makes real estate a powerful tool. In most businesses and investments, you may be paying 30–60 percent of your hard-earned money to the government. You are literally working the first half of the year to pay the government. With real estate and the right tax strategy, you can work the entire year for yourself.

TAX TENET #19

Document. Document. Document.

Benefits for All

You may be thinking that the tax benefits described in this chapter are only for real estate professionals or those who invest in and manage properties themselves. You would be sorely mistaken. Anyone investing in real estate can receive these benefits.

This includes making investments in your friend's real estate business or in a syndicated real estate deal with someone like my friend Ken McElroy. You will still need to pay attention to the passive activity rules described in Chapter 4. Regardless, if you invest in real estate in any way, you are likely to benefit from these tax incentives.

Chapter Summary

- ✓ *The government will reward real estate ownership over renting.*

- ✓ *The home sale exclusion can result in millions of tax-free dollars over your lifetime.*

- ✓ *1031 exchanges not only save you tax, but also increase your investment returns.*

- ✓ *The sale of real estate often results in the best of both worlds: capital gain and ordinary loss treatment.*

- ✓ *Depreciation is often recaptured at lower rates than the deduction.*

- ✓ *You can lose other people's money through depreciation deductions.*

- ✓ *Cash-out refinances are generally tax-free transactions.*

11

DON'T RELY ON
THE GOVERNMENT
TO RETIRE

The government and your employer love to push retirement plans on you. Why? Well, for many reasons. For one, they don't trust you to be able to retire on your own. But a big reason is because the government gets a return on your money when you use retirement plans.

Of course, the government isn't the only one feeding off your hard-earned money. Financial advisors, investment banks, money managers, and business owners can all make a killing if you decide to go into retirement accounts blindly. The market, the advisors, and banks don't care whether you make money on your investments because they make money on your fees regardless.

And don't forget that the income generated in your retirement account will be taxed at the higher ordinary income tax rates when you withdraw it in retirement, regardless of what kind of income could have been earned outside a retirement account.

If it seems I'm very negative toward retirement accounts, that's because I am. My prejudices against retirement accounts don't mean they don't have a use, but my advice is that you should exhaust all the other tax-advantaged avenues we have discussed in this book before considering a retirement account. Retirement accounts are great for business owners who have already maximized depreciation, utilized home office savings, converted personal expenses to business expenses, and employed the other strategies we have discussed. In other words, a retirement account should be the sidekick to all other tax planning strategies.

TAX TENET #20

Retirement accounts are an add-on, not the be-all and end-all.

With all that said, if you are an employee who chooses not to have a side business or invest in real estate, you will find retirement accounts useful. In fact, a retirement account will be one of your only options for reducing taxes by any meaningful amount.

STRATEGY TIP

To contribute to a retirement account, you need earned income. This means wages, salaries, or self-employment income. Contributions to retirement accounts are limited to the lessor of either your earned income or the specific limits on your type of retirement account.

Various Retirement Accounts

You have many options when it comes to retirement accounts. The main differences between them typically boil down to who is eligible and how much you can contribute each year. Contributions to retirement accounts other than Roth accounts provide a tax deduction, which is like an immediate tax benefit that allows you to invest more now.

Additionally, the investments made with your contributions will grow tax-deferred, meaning you will not pay tax on your contributions or earnings in the retirement account until you withdraw them in retirement. This puts the time value of money on your side as you're able to invest more dollars during your working years instead of paying larger sums in taxes. Most people will have a lower tax rate in retirement when the funds are withdrawn because their income is lower.

STRATEGY TIP

If you utilize the other strategies we've reviewed in this book, it's possible to have low taxable income in retirement even though your economic income is higher. Let that be your goal.

INDIVIDUAL RETIREMENT ACCOUNTS (IRAs)

These are very easy accounts to set up and most people can take advantage of them. However, the limits for annual contributions are the lowest of all the retirement account options. An IRA is a great option if you are not eligible for any of the other accounts or if you don't plan on contributing a significant amount or just want to use it as a supplement to another retirement account.

Your employer does not need to offer a retirement option for you to open an IRA. You also don't need your own business to contribute to these plans. You just need to make sure you have earned income, whether that comes from wages, salaries, or self-employment.

BEWARE

*Those who are eligible or have a spouse who is eligible for a **401(k)** retirement account through an employer may not be able to contribute to an IRA if their income is over certain thresholds. The annual contribution limits may also be reduced or completely phased out at higher income levels, depending on whether you have a traditional or Roth IRA.*

401(K)

401(k) retirement accounts are offered by many employers, and you should seriously consider taking advantage of such an offer. One benefit of a 401(k) over an IRA is that your employer can offer matching contributions, which means that for every dollar you contribute to the plan from your paycheck, your employer will contribute a percentage on your behalf. This has the effect of increasing your wages or salary, and it would be silly not to take advantage of this.

The annual contribution limits for a 401(k) are significantly higher than for IRAs. The limits for both types of accounts are adjusted each year, but the annual contribution limit for a 401(k) is about three and a half times greater than for IRAs. If you combine the matching benefits, which are a deduction for the employer, the annual limit is even greater.

These can be great plans for businesses that want to offer their employees a retirement option. A benefit of the 401(k) over some of the other plans for businesses is it allows employees to make contributions to the plan without requiring the employer to make additional contributions.

IN CASE OF AUDIT

Some retirement plans require more annual reporting than others. When you are choosing a retirement plan, consider the compliance needed and hire a professional who can stay on the ball.

SELF-EMPLOYED PENSION (SEP)

The **SEP** is a great plan for a single self-employed individual in a business. The limits for contributing are more than twice that of a 401(k), and it's much easier to set up. You can typically open this account on your own with an online broker, and there are no annual reporting requirements, which make this plan incredibly easy to maintain.

STRATEGY TIP

You typically do not want to set up a SEP retirement plan if you have employees because you will be required to contribute for every employee each year.

DEFINED BENEFIT PLANS

If you're a higher earner and want to stash away as much as possible into your retirement savings, this is the plan for you. It's the type of plan most doctors, attorneys, CPAs, and similar professionals will use.

A ***defined benefit plan*** is very different from the other plans in the sense that the employer is guaranteeing an amount at retirement. In other words, you are making contributions so the participants will receive a specific amount in retirement. The other retirement plans discussed here are ***defined contribution plans,*** meaning you can contribute certain amounts each year, but there's no guarantee what amount will be received in retirement. The benefits from a defined contribution plan will be determined based on the contributions and the earnings on those contributions.

The main benefit of defined benefit plans is the ability to contribute significantly more than other plans, which is what makes this type of plan great for high earners who plan to invest in items that make sense for a retirement account. This usually isn't a great plan if you have other employees in the business unless you keep the defined benefit plan in a separate taxable entity from the main business that has the employees.

STRATEGY TIP

Most of these retirement plans allow you to make contributions after the tax year. For example, if you want to make a contribution for the 2024 tax year, you may be able to contribute until as late as October 15, 2025. This is one of the few tax planning strategies you can implement after year-end!

CHOOSE WISELY

The plans listed above are not the only retirement plans available, but they are the most common by far. The biggest deciding factors in choosing a plan are:

- Whether you have employees and want them to have the ability to make retirement contributions;

- Whether you have employees and want to contribute to their retirement plans on their behalf;

- How much you plan to contribute each year; and

- How much annual reporting you are willing to undertake.

> ### STRATEGY TIP
> *A 10 percent penalty will be added on the amount withdrawn from a retirement plan before you hit age fifty-nine and one-half. Many retirement plans will allow exemptions from this penalty if the withdrawn funds are used for a specific purpose like education or medical expenses.*

Traditional vs. Roth

In addition to the retirement accounts presented previously, many retirement accounts can be either a traditional type retirement account or a **Roth retirement account.** When deciding between contributing to a traditional or a Roth, you are deciding between pre-tax or after-tax dollars. **Traditional retirement accounts** provide for a deduction against your income when you make contributions to them. This means that traditional retirement accounts are pre-tax. The retirement earnings will also grow tax-deferred over the life of the retirement account. Notice, however, these are not tax-free.

When the funds are withdrawn from a traditional IRA, you will owe tax at your marginal tax bracket.

A Roth retirement account is the opposite. Contributions to a Roth account do not generate a tax deduction. Instead, you pay tax on your contributions, but you will not owe any tax on money you withdraw from a Roth in retirement. That means the earnings in a Roth will grow tax-free, not **tax-deferred.**

Choosing whether to invest in a traditional account or a Roth account is not always straightforward. There are many factors to consider, in addition to the fact that we can't predict future tax rates with certainty. However, the two most important factors in making this decision are what you expect your future tax rate will be compared to what it is now and how long until you expect to retire. See Table 11.1 for simplified decision-making advice.

Table 11.1. Retirement account choices

Choose	Traditional	Roth
If	You expect your tax bracket to be lower in retirement	You expect your tax bracket to be higher in retirement
	Shorter period until retirement	Longer period until retirement

USING ROTH CONVERSIONS TO CREATE TAX-FREE MONEY

Most people don't see steady increases in their incomes every year over their lifetimes. There may be large increases and large decreases. This is especially true for business owners experiencing economic cycles or other changes in the business environment. It can also be true for people who switch jobs or career paths, go back to school, pause their career to take care of children, or find themselves in a variety of other circumstances.

A Roth conversion allows you to take advantage of these changes in your income levels and therefore your tax rates. If you have a traditional IRA, you can convert it to a Roth retirement account; since you would be converting from a pretax account to an after-tax account, you will have to pay tax on the amount that you convert.

You may have decided to contribute to a traditional IRA when your income was high, which allowed you to receive large tax savings for those contributions, in anticipation that they would be taxed at a lower rate in retirement after growing tax-deferred for many years. However, if your income drops substantially before retirement, this could be the perfect time to convert those IRA dollars to a Roth account. You would pay tax on the amount converted to the Roth based on your tax bracket in the year of conversion, but it allows your future earnings to grow absolutely tax-free, as is illustrated in Table 11.2!

To see how this could work to your benefit, let's assume you have a $100,000 traditional IRA that you contributed to when you were in a high tax bracket. After five years, you find yourself in a transitionary period where your tax rate is much lower. You could convert all $100,000 from a traditional IRA to a Roth and pay taxes at only a 12 percent rate. Converting to a Roth would mean you would pay $12,000 in tax ($100,000 x 12 percent), which—for the purpose of this illustration—you pay from other sources so you could convert the full $100,000 into the Roth.

Table 11.2. Comparing retirement account results

	Traditional	Roth
Year 1	$100,000	$100,000
Year 40	$4,114,478	$4,114,478
Tax owed in retirement	$1,028,619	$0
Net value	$3,085,858	$4,114,478

Assuming a 10 percent compounded annual return, both a traditional and a Roth account starting at $100,000 would grow to a little over $4.1 million. If you had a 25 percent tax bracket in retirement, you would owe a little over $1 million in tax for a traditional retirement account and no tax for a Roth retirement account. That is a $1,000,000 benefit for simply making a Roth conversion in a low tax rate year and paying $12,000 in taxes that year!

Use Retirement Accounts to Your Advantage

Invest in assets that will generate ordinary income. The best investments for retirement accounts are treasury bonds, tax liens, real estate loans, and stocks held for short-term capital gains.

Many retirement plans will allow you to make loans to yourself, which can be a lucrative way to lower your taxes. A loan will generate ordinary interest income for the retirement plan and allow you to make investments in assets that will generate capital gains outside of the plan. Many plans will allow you to take an even bigger loan if it's to purchase your principal residence.

Note that each retirement plan has different rules around loans or whether you can take a loan at all. Check with your employer and plan administrator before counting on this strategy.

STRATEGY TIP

If you invest in assets that would generate capital gains with a retirement account, you are converting income that could be taxed at 0 percent to 20 percent preferential rates to ordinary income rates as high as 37 percent (for 2024). To avoid this, invest in ordinary income items through the retirement account and keep capital gain items and tax-exempt investments (i.e. tax-exempt municipal bonds) outside your retirement account.

Why I Don't Like Using Retirement Accounts for Real Estate

In case it wasn't clear when I said in the last chapter that real estate is the wealthy person's treasure chest, I'm going to reiterate it here. Where else in the tax law can you get a reduction in your taxes for actually increasing your wealth!?

However, investing in real estate through a retirement account would be the same as signing up for a gym membership and never working out. You will have sheathed your greatest weapon. In Figure 11.1 I explain my three biggest objections to investing in real estate through a retirement account.

Figure 11.1. Three big reasons why real estate and retirement accounts should not mix

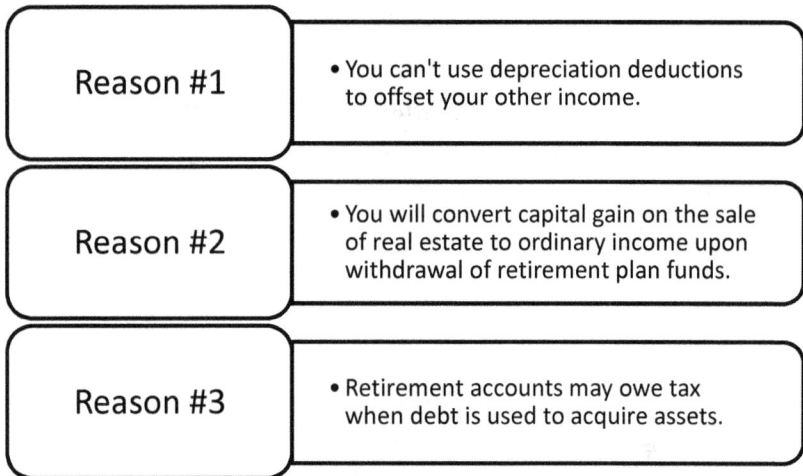

Reason #1	• You can't use depreciation deductions to offset your other income.
Reason #2	• You will convert capital gain on the sale of real estate to ordinary income upon withdrawal of retirement plan funds.
Reason #3	• Retirement accounts may owe tax when debt is used to acquire assets.

STRATEGY TIP

You can invest in real estate using certain retirement accounts that will not generate tax from assets acquired with debt. Make sure to check with your CPA if this is something you're considering.

Clients often ask me about using self-directed IRAs for real estate investment, and such retirement accounts certainly have their place. However, I always advise my clients to consider the types of investments very carefully. If you're thinking about doing this, get advice from an unbiased party before setting up one of these accounts.

Strategy for Retirees

It's very possible to have income in retirement and still pay zero taxes. This feat can even be achieved without owning real estate or using the other strategies outlined previously. In fact, if you are a typical wage earner who is receiving Social Security and retirement distributions and have an investment portfolio outside of your retirement accounts, the following strategy is perfect for you.

Favorable Factors for Retirees

Many factors work in favor of retirees when it comes to taxes.

- *Social Security benefits are not always subject to taxes. In fact, the taxable portion ranges between 0 percent and 85 percent depending on your combined income and your filing status.*

- *Capital gains rates range from 0 percent in the lowest tax brackets to 20 percent in the highest tax brackets.*

- *You probably won't have many itemized deductions since most retirees will want to pay off their principal residence by the time they retire. In this case, retirees will still receive the freebie standard deduction.*

- *If you have a Roth retirement account, the distributions from that account won't be considered when determining how much of your Social Security benefits and capital gain income are taxable. This is because distributions from Roth retirement accounts are not taxable when withdrawn.*

The way you accomplish zero taxes is by maximizing the amount of Social Security benefits with capital gain income. You will only have a certain amount of control over your Social Security benefit amount so you'll want to figure out that amount first. Once you've determined how much you will receive in Social Security benefits for the year, you can layer on capital gains.

To generate capital gains, you can invest in dividend income stocks through your taxable investment portfolio. You'll want to make sure they will be qualified dividends; otherwise, the dividends won't be taxed as capital gain income. If done correctly, any taxable portion of your Social Security benefits will be wiped out by your standard deduction, and the capital gain income above the standard deduction will be taxed at zero percent.

For 2024, a married couple filing jointly can make up to around $100,000 in Social Security benefits and capital gain income without paying any tax. Of course, this amount will change each year and will greatly depend on the relative amount of Social Security benefits to capital gain income. Work with your tax advisor for the optimal amount of capital gain income depending on your situation.

After you've maximized your Social Security benefits and capital gain income for zero tax, in come the Roth distributions. You can use tax-free Roth distributions to make up the difference between what you're receiving in Social Security and capital gains to what you need to live the lifestyle you want in retirement.

Chapter Summary

✓ *Do not invest in real estate or tax-exempt income through a retirement account.*

✓ *By using Roth conversions, you can create tax-free income in retirement.*

✓ *You should consider exhausting other tax-planning techniques before maximizing your retirement contributions.*

✓ *Retirees can pay zero tax by optimizing their Social Security benefits, capital gain income, and retirement plan distributions.*

12

HEIR-ING ON THE SIDE OF GENERATIONAL WEALTH

Many people think accumulating wealth is so difficult that they never stop to consider the challenges they might face once they have wealth. Sure, we've all heard the phrase, "mo' money, mo' problems," but what does that really mean?

Surely the ability to afford better health care, take more vacations, and enjoy financial freedom can't actually be more problematic. And honestly, it *should be* less problematic. However, if you don't plan well while you're accumulating your wealth, taxes will become a big problem after you've got it.

Imagine working your entire adult life, making sacrifices, delaying your dreams, and finally achieving your financial goals, but then half of your wealth disappears before you can pass it on to your heirs. Generational wealth becomes a huge consideration for those who have wealth and a family or a great cause they would like to share it with.

Family dynamics can be difficult. Your spouse and your heirs will be different from anyone else's, so the financial considerations associated with your family will be unique too. My father always told my sister and me, "Don't expect to get anything from us as an inheritance. Your mom and I are going to spend it all on travel and enjoying our lives." Ultimately, he wanted to make us self-sufficient and ensure we would not be waiting around to be handed anything.

That approach works with some children, but definitely not all. Even siblings from the same parents will vary greatly in financial mindset, knowledge, and motivations. This will be the same for anyone with children, grandchildren, or anyone else they are considering passing their wealth to. You will certainly want to consider your own family dynamics and work with your CPA and estate attorney to devise a plan that works best for everyone.

If you're getting close to this stage, I would strongly encourage you to do some in-depth reading and research on this topic. In this section I aim to provide overall tax concepts you should consider as part of a generational wealth plan. But you will do best getting personalized advice too.

There are two main considerations regarding estate and gift taxation. First, there are the income tax considerations. Income tax has been the main focus of this book, and obviously, income tax is based on earned income. The second major consideration that comes into play with estate tax planning is the actual **estate tax.** This is a tax on the value of an individual's estate at the time of death. Rather than being based on income, it's based on value.

TAX TENET #21

Generational planning is critical for tax avoidance.

Death Step-Up

This might sound terrible, but one of the greatest tax planning techniques is dying. When you are alive, you will generally pay income tax when you sell assets for more than your cost basis. However, when you die, the IRS allows your heirs to make a "step up" in basis of those assets equal to the fair market value at the date of your death. This means your cost basis now becomes the same as the current fair market value. If those assets are sold immediately or before the fair market value changes, there will be no income tax paid on those gains.

STRATEGY TIP

If you live in a community property state and one spouse passes away, all of the community property, including the surviving spouse's portion, will receive a step-up in tax basis to the fair market value. In this case, avoid selling appreciated assets before one spouse passes to eliminate the income tax.

The step-up rule is a great reason to hold appreciated assets in your portfolio and let your heirs sell them after you die. Otherwise, you will owe income tax when you sell, thereby reducing the amount that goes to your heirs.

STRATEGY TIP

I had a client who had invested in real estate for most of his life. He made frequent 1031 exchanges to defer the taxes. Eventually, like everyone, he passed away. His strategy was great for his heirs, though, because he converted what would have been a huge tax liability from years of deferring taxes through 1031s to tax-free income by passing away when still holding those low-cost-basis assets. His actions meant his heirs paid no income tax on years of deferred income.

TAX TENET #22

Death is a tax planning tool.

Estates and the Lifetime Exemption

Income tax is only half the battle. The government also applies a tax to the net value of your estate. If you're subject to this tax, your heirs will feel the pain, especially if the estate is subject to the highest tax rate, which is currently 37 percent. Lucky for your kids, there is a break for estates under the **lifetime exemption.** Estates that are below the lifetime exemption are not subject to the estate tax.

The lifetime exemption allows taxpayers to give gifts during their lifetime and to transfer wealth upon death. This amount is adjusted for inflation each year and changes based on acts of Congress. For 2024, the lifetime exemption amount is $13.61 million for each taxpayer. You'll want to keep an eye on this amount because it's expected to drop significantly starting in tax year 2026, and this expected change makes the next few years critical for estate planning if you have anywhere near this amount of net worth or more.

IN CASE OF AUDIT

For many assets, you'll want to get an appraisal for the estate. This will make sure you have a defense against the IRS if they try to argue a different value, which is typically higher than what you want it to be. This is one way the IRS attacks large estates.

Gifting and the Annual Exclusion

Gifts are not taxable to the recipient. When you gift assets that are appreciated, the recipient will receive those gifts at the same cost basis as the transferor had. For example, if you gift a stock worth $10,000 that you bought for $4,000 five years ago, the recipient's tax basis in the stock will be $4,000. The recipient will not pay any tax at the time the stock is received, but if they sell the stock while its value is $10,000, they will pay tax on the $6,000 gain. In this case, the amount treated as a gift for the transferor is the fair market value or $10,000, even though the tax basis may be lower.

The transferor will only owe tax on gifts if those gifts exceed either their annual exclusion or lifetime exemption, mentioned previously. The annual gift exclusion for 2024 is $18,000. A taxpayer can gift up to this amount each year to a single recipient without owing tax or reducing their lifetime exemption.

STRATEGY TIP

The annual exclusion is per recipient. If you are not married and have two children, you can gift $18,000 to each of them without any tax consequences. If you give one of them any amount over this in a year, you will reduce your lifetime exemption, but you will not owe tax until your lifetime exemption is reduced to zero. The current lifetime exemption is $13.61 million.

THE INTERPLAY BETWEEN GIFTS AND THE LIFETIME EXEMPTION

If you gift more than the annual exclusion in any given tax year, the amount that is in excess will go against the lifetime exemption allowed. The lifetime exemption reduced by gifts during your lifetime that exceeded the annual exclusion is the remaining lifetime exemption. The remaining lifetime exemption at the time of death is the amount that will determine whether your estate is subject to the estate tax. Estates with a total value of less than the remaining lifetime exemption will not be subject to the estate tax.

BEWARE

Each state has its own rules on how estates will be taxed. The general rules in this chapter cover the federal tax consequences for estates. Some states do not have an estate tax, while others follow the federal rules, and yet others have their own rules. You'll need to check in your specific state to know how they treat estates for tax purposes.

Remove Assets from Your Taxable Estate

When you are approaching a net worth that is near the lifetime exemption, you should focus on removing as many assets out of your estate as possible. You can accomplish this by gifting directly to your heirs or by gifting to trusts with your heirs as beneficiaries. The latter allows you to control those assets during your lifetime and control the amount received by your heirs after death. This is a great tool for generational wealth.

BEWARE

Assets that are gifted using certain trusts will not receive the step-up in tax basis. The only assets that will receive a step-up in basis are those that are in your estate at the time of death.

The main benefit of gifting assets to trusts during your lifetime is removing all the future appreciation of those assets from your estate. For example, let's assume you have assets of $10 million and that these are appreciating assets like real estate. Assuming you have not reduced your lifetime exemption, you could gift all these assets to a trust with your heirs as the beneficiaries. This would be a tax-free transaction. At this point, these assets are no longer in your taxable estate. The incredible part is all these assets can grow free of the estate tax. If the assets grow to $20 million by the time you pass away, none of these assets will be subject to the high estate tax despite being in excess of the lifetime exemption.

STRATEGY TIP

Work with an estate attorney to set up the correct type of trust for your situation. Gifting to certain trusts does not remove assets from your taxable estate.

When your estate is already over the lifetime exemption or you have already maximized the lifetime exemption, there are still some ways to transfer some or all of your estate tax-free.

The first and most obvious is to max out the annual gift exclusion for each of your heirs, each year. This will slowly remove assets from your taxable estate and won't cause any tax consequences for you or your heirs.

Another strategy, which I personally love because it may also teach your heirs financial independence, is to involve them in your business. You can pay your heirs to work in your business. In addition to removing those amounts from your estate, your business can receive a deduction for those wages. Talk about killing two birds with one stone! Further, if you don't pay more than the standard deduction applicable to your heirs each year and they have no other income; your heirs won't pay tax on those wages.

For a single taxpayer, the standard deduction in 2024 is $14,600. This means you can pay your child this amount before they owe any tax and your business will receive a deduction. Combine this with the $18,000 annual exclusion and you can reduce your estate by $32,600 for each child with no negative tax consequences. Your children will also learn to work in the business. If you're getting any funny ideas, read that last sentence again. Your children must be performing a function in the business for you to write off a paycheck to them. You cannot simply pay them for doing nothing. You also need to make sure you pay a market rate for the work they perform. This is an all-around great estate planning strategy.

I've covered some very advanced tax and estate topics in just a few short words. You will definitely want to work with your estate attorney and CPA before trying any of these strategies on your own. If you have a large estate, the strategies I've described are only a teaser for what estate planning possibilities exist. You'll want to make sure to reference TaxStrategiesForEveryone.com for changes to the annual gifting exclusion and the lifetime exemption.

IN CASE OF AUDIT

When gifting above the annual exclusion, a gift tax return is required. This is a separate tax return from your individual income tax return. Make sure to tell your CPA about any gifts in advance so this is handled correctly. Missing a tax filing can mean the statute of limitations doesn't start running.

Chapter Summary

✓ *You need to consider both the income tax and the estate tax when making your estate plan.*

✓ *Assets held by your estate will receive a death step-up to their fair market value that eliminates any income tax liability that grew during your lifetime.*

✓ *Use gifting strategies to remove assets from your taxable estate if you will be close to or over the lifetime exemption.*

✓ *Tax years 2024 through 2025 will be critical for estate planning because the lifetime exemption is expected to drop.*

✓ *Making annual gifts and paying salaries to your heirs can help reduce your taxable estate.*

✓ *Gifts are not taxable to the recipient.*

13

WHO CAN YOU TRUST?

When it comes to taxes, your tax savings can only be as good as your tax advisor. You'll want to spend some time and energy up front to make sure you draft the best tax advisor for your team. Finding the right advisor can be challenging because the best fit for your friend or neighbor or father-in-law is not necessarily the best fit for you. There are, however, some general guidelines you can follow to ensure your search is successful.

It's not your responsibility to know every nuance of the U.S. federal tax law or how it might affect you. Your job is to focus on your business, your job, your finances, and the other details of living the best life you can. To ensure you're living your best life, you should be sure you understand the basics of tax law—which you are obviously doing by reading this book!

But for anything beyond the basics, you need a good tax advisor. And it's your responsibility to hire the best tax advisor for your situation. This can be a daunting task, and I'll tell you why.

In the very general sense, tax advisors are like any other professional: some know what they are doing and take pride in their work, and some don't. This holds true for brokers, financial planners, architects, engineers, tradesmen, restaurant owners, and any other profession you can think of. It can be difficult to identify which professionals have the necessary skills, ethics, and sense of responsibility when you don't know what you're looking for.

Understanding the concepts presented in this book will help you vet a potential tax advisor. You can more easily interpret what they present to you and whether their information seems accurate.

And this chapter will provide you with more information about finding the best tax advisor for you. When you complete this chapter, you will know what questions to ask and what red flags to avoid. This chapter is the final step in your journey of making the best tax decisions possible.

TAX TENET #23

Not all tax advisors are created equal.

Assess Your Needs

You cannot skip this step if you want to end up with the best tax advisor from a cost/benefit analysis. Unless you're a large corporation, likely publicly traded, you would be wasting your resources to hire a **Big Four** tax firm. You just won't need the expertise that you would be paying for from these professionals. It would be overkill.

On the other hand, if you run a successful business, you also don't want to use a volume producer like H&R Block, Liberty Tax, or Turbo Tax. The professionals working for these companies simply won't have the expertise to advise you on your best tax moves. You will probably end up paying more unnecessary taxes than any savings you might get from a lower tax preparation bill. And you're not likely to get much good advice either.

Figure 13.1 displays some information to help you decide on the right type of firm for you. It's organized from bottom to top, going from the least costly service and the lowest knowledge base to the most expensive and highest competency level.

Figure 13.1. The rising expertise—and cost—of tax professionals

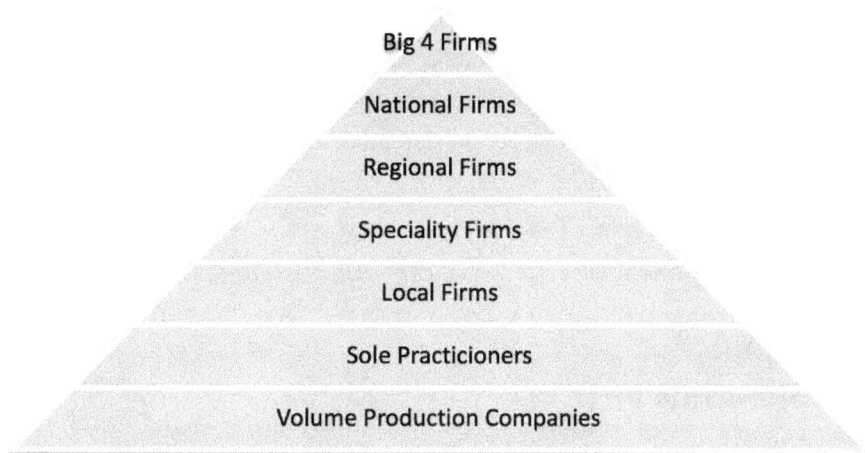

Big 4 Firms

National Firms

Regional Firms

Speciality Firms

Local Firms

Sole Practicioners

Volume Production Companies

Frankly, Bad Advice Can Cost You Dearly

A few years ago, I received a call from a gentleman—let's call him Frank—who had seen me on YouTube. Frank was a real estate investor focusing mainly on shopping centers who had been working with a local CPA in his state. As I listened to Frank's story, it was clear that he was focused on keeping his costs low, especially the costs he didn't really value. One of these costs was tax preparation and consulting.

It was clear from everything Frank told me that he was a real estate professional whose wife had a good-paying job. I asked Frank to send me his tax returns so I could see how his CPA was preparing them. It turned out the CPA was not treating him as a real estate professional, which meant he wasn't deducting Frank's real estate loss against his wife's high-paying W-2 job.

I instantly saw the potential for amending Frank's returns and getting him large refunds, in the area of $40,000. To top it off, his CPA had never suggested performing a cost segregation study on his properties. I could tell doing this would completely offset all his wife's income. Following these steps would enable Frank to go from paying upward of $100,000 a year in taxes to absolutely nothing! Frank was really missing out.

More often than not, business owners are working with tax professionals who aren't qualified to handle their tax details. This is one of many times when cutting costs can end up costing far more in tax. Be aware that small local companies may not have the specific industry expertise to properly advise a business owner.

TAX TENET #24

Cut costs, but don't cut off your nose to spite your face.

Get Referrals First

A lot of CPAs probably don't appreciate me saying this, but CPAs are humans, not spreadsheet machines. Oh, and most CPAs aren't very confrontational. (Sometimes stereotypes are true.) In interviews, they are likely to agree with you and tell you what you want to hear because they want to make you happy. (Sorry, fellow CPAs, for the overgeneralization.) Just know that a person's performance during the interview process is not always an indicator of actual performance. This happens with traditional employees as well as with CPAs or other tax advisors.

A good way to measure potential performance is to solicit referrals. Your friends, business associates, business partners, etc., will likely know, know of, or have worked with someone who worked with a CPA. Get their information and contact those referrals first. You are much more likely to receive unbiased feedback on an advisor's prior history. Think of it as doing a reference check on potential employees—which your tax advisor will be.

IN CASE OF AUDIT

The correct tax advisor can do wonders for preventing an unnecessary audit.

Specific Knowledge Is Valuable

A developer we will call Alan had been working well with another tax professional for over ten years, so he didn't hesitate to call his longtime advisor to help with a **qualified opportunity zone** project. Well, it only took one major deadline missed and a $100K penalty notice from the IRS for Alan and his attorney to realize they needed to bring in a tax advisor who could help navigate the unique rules of opportunity zones.

I had been working with opportunity zones for a couple years at this point, and I was able to navigate the rules and get penalties removed for Alan after he called me. Everyone learned an important lesson from this event.

Although Alan's advisor was very experienced and knowledge-able, he did not have any other clients with an opportunity zone project. The tax code and regulations on Alan's project went on for hundreds of pages and it wasn't even finalized law, so it was con-stantly changing during this initial period.

You could be working with a great professional, but if you're running a business, you need someone who knows the specific rules related to your industry. I wish I could say that I know everything, but I don't. Anyone who claims they know it all is lying.

Make sure you have someone who regularly works in your industry or within the area of the tax law where you need exper-tise. This can literally save you hundreds of thousands of dollars, as it did Alan.

A CPA Should Help Build Your Team

I want you to think of your CPA as your partner. Now, I don't mean you have to share your profits with your CPA. However, as your business grows and your needs expand, you will need additional expertise. Remember what I said about how great referrals can jump-start your business? Well, your CPA can do the same thing for you.

I can't tell you how many times my friend, and client, Ken McElroy has asked if I know anyone in a particular field. A couple years ago, I was helping Ken make some pretty big tax moves that were going to make a big difference to his estate plan. He had an attorney for his business but not one who had the specific expertise needed to execute this plan. (Cue reminder that specific knowledge is valuable.)

It just so happened that I knew the perfect attorney for the job. I knew this attorney was knowledgeable in the specific area Ken needed because you can't fake it when you work with someone. My knowledge saved Ken from needing to interview a half dozen attorneys and still wonder whether any of them would perform well. Not only that, but I was the one who would be working closely with the attorney. You think Ken wanted to be involved in all the legal and tax mumbo jumbo? No, he wanted to understand the big picture and rely on a team he could trust. This was invaluable to him.

A well-connected CPA should be able to link you up with a whole host of professionals you might need in your business. This isn't an exhaustive list but should give you some insight into the potential connections you could make through your CPA.

- Attorneys
- Real estate brokers
- Business brokers
- Financial planners
- Financial managers
- Property managers
- Insurance agents
- Bankers
- Lenders

- **Payroll providers**

- **Cost segregation experts (If your CPA doesn't do this themselves)**

The list goes on and on. These professionals know your CPA is a valuable resource also. Guess who is trying to go to lunch with me all the time and is constantly sending me marketing materials and gift baskets? That's right, all the people in the industries listed above. They want an in with a good CPA because they know the CPA's clients will need these kinds of professionals.

But I don't refer people just because they sent me a nice bottle of wine. I only refer professionals I am confident can do a good job, and your CPA should be doing the same. Your CPA should be familiar with a professional's knowledge, skill level, experience, and work before referring them to you.

No Questions Should Be a Red Flag

I hope you realize by now how complex the tax laws are. And honestly, this book doesn't even scratch the surface. It's not your job to know all the different nuances and scenarios. That's your advisor's responsibility. But how would you expect your advisor to find tax benefits and loopholes for you if they don't ask you questions? They need to ask questions. Lots of them. Lots of pointed questions. Otherwise, you will never know what information you need to share.

A good rule of thumb is that for every question you ask your advisor, they should be asking you one to five questions in response. If they have a simple answer for all your questions, they probably aren't digging deep enough. I'm not saying your advisor will always find a way to get the result you want, but you need to be assured that they are working hard at it.

If you're interviewing a potential tax advisor who isn't asking you questions, walk away. Immediately. This isn't the advisor for you.

TAX TENET #25

A good CPA is a curious CPA.

Be a Part of Your Tax Decisions

This might seem obvious, but you need to understand what your CPA is saying to you. Often, when I'm speaking with a potential client or consulting with a client, they tell me they have taken a particular action because "my CPA said I need to do this." When I ask them why, they frequently say, "I don't know. The CPA never said *why* to do it that way."

A lot of CPAs may not know how to translate technical tax talk into layman's terms, and too often they will say something to the effect of "It's what's best" when they aren't interested in truly explaining a piece of advice. Don't let your advisor off the hook that easily.

You need to be on the same page with your advisor as far as your goals and the actions that will get you there. If you don't know why you're doing something, you can't be sure that specific move will fit your goals. If your CPA isn't interested in explaining anything to you, move on. You may not need to know all the technical details of a move, but you do need to be aware of the benefits and the potential pitfalls because there are many good tax moves that can still have risks or downsides.

Hopefully by now you see how important it is to have the right tax advisor on your team. The task may have seemed daunting at the beginning, but by applying the principles we have explored in this chapter, you'll make the task much simpler.

A good tax advisor can save you thousands, hundreds of thousands, or even millions of dollars in taxes. A poor tax advisor can cost you the same. Put the work in at the beginning because sometimes it's too late to correct this mistake.

Chapter Summary

✓ *Your tax savings are only as good as your tax advisor's skills.*

✓ *Everyone will have specific needs and, therefore, the best tax advisor for you will depend on your goals and circumstances.*

✓ *Your tax advisor is part of your team, so treat them that way.*

✓ *The size and specific knowledge of a tax business is critical to your decision.*

✓ *Pay attention to whether a tax professional asks you questions.*

✓ *Don't turn a blind eye to your tax moves; understand them.*

LET'S WRAP UP THIS SNOOZEFEST

After reading this book, you should have learned many tax-saving strategies you can implement whether you're an employee, a retiree, self-employed, investor or a business owner. There are many more opportunities beyond the context of this book that could apply to you. This is only a stepping stone on your journey to significant tax savings.

If you don't remember everything you've read here, that's okay. In fact, I wouldn't expect you to. But I hope you will remember the value principle: that is, if you create community value, you can save on taxes. This is the theme of the federal tax code and a priority of the U.S. government. Keep this principle as a reference point and reminder as you make business and financial decisions.

Another important tax principle I want you to remember: it depends. Because of that principle, it's important for you to consult with a qualified professional before implementing any of the strategies in this book. There are many pitfalls to be wary of and many other possibilities that we didn't have a chance to cover. I encourage you to read more in-depth on the topics presented in this book and bring your questions to your tax advisor. Have an open dialogue and truly treat your advisor as part of your team.

Taxes will likely be the largest expense of your lifetime. But this is an expense you can take control over. You can choose to pay more than your fair share, or you can choose to be proactive and seek ways to minimize your tax bill. Many people forget that tax planning should be a critical part of any financial plan, but readers of this book won't fall into that trap. If the information and insight you discover in these pages allows you to reach your financial goals more easily, then I will have fulfilled my goals for writing this book.

GLOSSARY

1031 exchange: A tax-deferred sale of real property when like-kind property is acquired following the rules of Internal Revenue Code Section 1031.

401(k): A retirement account often offered by employers that allows employees to contribute from their earnings and allows investment income to grow tax-free or tax-deferred, depending on whether it's a traditional or Roth account.

above the line deduction: These deductions come before the adjusted gross income (AGI) line on your tax return.

adjusted basis: The cost basis adjusted for various items such as depreciation or improvements.

adjusted gross income (AGI): A defining line on your tax return that separates above the line deductions from below the line deductions.

annuity: A contract for a fixed sum of payments to be made.

average tax rate: The amount of tax you owe divided by your taxable income. (See "effective tax rate")

below the line deduction: A deduction that comes after the AGI line on your tax return.

Big Four: Describes the four largest accounting firms by revenue.

boot: Property received in a 1031 exchange that is not considered like-kind and may result in a taxable exchange.

business income: Income earned from a business that is not self-employment income.

business miles: The miles driven that are considered for business as defined by the Internal Revenue Code.

capital gain: The difference between what you sell a capital asset for and your adjusted basis.

cash flow: The cash inflows minus the cash outflows during a specified period.

C-corporation: A tax designation recognized by the Internal Revenue Code.

cost basis: Typically, the amount paid for an asset, plus any acquisition costs.

cost segregation: A tax strategy that separates the different components of an asset into shorter, useful lives. This allows you to accelerate depreciation deductions.

death step-up: When assets in your estate receive an increase to their tax basis based on the fair market value at the time of death.

deduction: a reduction of your taxable income.

defined benefit plan: A retirement plan you make contributions to in order to receive a certain amount in retirement. You back into the contribution amounts based on what you are expected to receive in retirement.

defined contribution plan: A retirement plan where contributions are made without regard to how much will be received in retirement.

depreciable basis: The amount you are allowed to take depreciation deductions from.

depreciating asset: An asset that loses value over time.

depreciation: The deduction of an asset's depreciable basis over multiple years.

depreciation recapture: The application of a higher tax rate when an asset that has been depreciated is disposed of for more than its adjusted basis.

depreciation schedule: A schedule tracking the cost basis and depreciation deductions for assets.

dividend: The distribution of corporate profits.

earned income: Income received from a salary, wage, or self-employment.

economic income: When the actual value of what you own increases.

economic loss: When the actual value of what you own decreases.

effective tax rate: The amount of tax you owe divided by your taxable income. (See "average tax rate")

eligible education institution: A school offering education beyond high school. Tuition and related expenses paid to these institutions may be eligible for tax credits or deductions.

employee: Someone working for a business for wages or salary who is subject to significant control from the employer regarding when and how specific tasks will be completed. Employees are on an employer's payroll and receive a Form W-2 at the end of the year.

equity: Assets less liabilities.

estate tax: A tax on the value of a deceased person's net worth.

ex-dividend date: One market day before the record date.

federal income tax: Tax the federal government charges on the income you earn. It is collected by the IRS.

general partner: Individual or entity who manages the entity's business affairs. This partner will make most day-to-day decisions but may need support of limited partner(s) for major decisions.

general partnership: A partnership made up of at least two partners. All partners have unlimited liability for debts and other obligations of the partnership.

gross income: Income before any deductions or taxes.

home office deduction: A deduction for using your home as an office.

independent contractor: A person who performs work for a business but is not subject to control from the employer regarding when and how specific tasks are completed. Independent contractors earning $600 or more will receive a 1099 at the end of the year.

individual retirement account (IRA): A retirement account allowing the deferral of tax on earnings until retirement.

interest: Income earned for allowing the use of money.

itemized deduction: Deductions that are personal in nature and deducted below the AGI line.

lifestyle deductions: Deductions that would otherwise be personal but become deductible when connected to a business purpose.

lifetime exemption: An amount that marks the cutoff between nontaxable and taxable gifts and estates.

limited liability company (LLC): An entity created within a state that is made up of members and managers and includes at least one member. The members and managers have limited liability.

limited liability limited partnership (LLLP): This entity is considered a hybrid of the limited partnership and the limited liability partnership. In this structure, there is at least one general partner and one limited partner, similar to an LP. However, unlike in an LP, the general partner will generally not be subject to the debts of the partnership.

limited liability partnership (LLP): A type of partnership created within a state that is made up of two or more limited partners. The limited partners have limited liability.

limited partner: Individual or entity who is not actively involved in the day-to-day management of the entity but may still retain voting rights on major decisions.

limited partnership (LP): A type of partnership created within a state which is made up of at least one general partner and one limited partner. The general partners have unlimited liability, and limited partners have limited liability.

marginal tax bracket: The highest rate of tax paid on your ordinary income.

modified accelerated cost recovery system: A depreciation method allowed for certain assets allowing you to receive deductions at a faster rate.

ordinary income: Income that receives no preferential, or reduced, tax rate.

organizational expenses: Costs incurred with setting up a business, including legal organization, agreements, and other related expenses.

partnership: A tax designation recognized by the Internal Revenue Code when an entity includes multiple owners.

passive income: Income earned from sources defined as passive by the Internal Revenue Code.

personal income: Income earned from the sale of personal assets, not connected with a business or a job.

placed in service: When an asset is first available for use and may be depreciated, if applicable.

portfolio income: Typically interest, dividends, and capital gains.

property tax: A tax based on the value of your real estate property or personal property. Typically, the tax on owning personal property will only apply to businesses.

qualified business income deduction (QBID): A deduction allowed for individuals and trusts and estates. The deduction is up to a maximum of 20 percent of qualified business income.

qualified dividend: Corporate distributions from a stock that you have held for sixty days before the ex-dividend date. These dividends are eligible for preferential tax rates.

qualified improvement property: Property that may be allowed faster depreciation and may be eligible for bonus depreciation and Section 179.

qualified opportunity zone: A special provision in the Internal Revenue Code that allows tax benefits for making investments in specific zones.

realized gain: Occurs when an asset is sold for more than its adjusted basis. The gain may or may not be subject to tax depending on whether it is also a recognized gain.

recognized gain: A realized gain that is also subject to tax.

record date: The date a shareholder must be in the corporate books to receive a dividend.

relinquished property: The property sold in a 1031 exchange.

rental income: Income received for allowing the use of your property to others.

replacement property: The property purchased in a 1031 exchange.

roth retirement account: A retirement account that does not allow for a tax deduction of contributions. Earnings will grow tax-free, and funds are not subject to tax when withdrawn.

royalty: A sum of money paid to a patentee, author, composer, or similar for a work, typically as a percentage of revenue.

salary: An amount paid to an employee over time based on their job responsibilities.

sales tax: Consumption-based tax, meaning you pay based on the amount you spend. Different rates apply in different states, cities, and local jurisdictions. You'll see this tax detailed on most receipts when you make a purchase.

S-corporation: A tax designation recognized by the Internal Revenue Code.

self-employed pension (SEP): A retirement plan for self-employed individuals allowing the deferral of taxes on earnings until retirement.

self-employment income: Income subject to the self-employment tax.

self-employment tax: Tax collected specifically to fund Social Security and Medicare. Self-employment tax is collected by the IRS and will be reported on your federal income tax return.

sole proprietorship: A tax designation recognized by the Internal Revenue Code when there is one owner.

standard deduction: A below the line deduction allowed for individual taxpayers based on their filing status.

start-up expenses: Costs incurred before doors open for business.

state income tax: A state government's version of federal income tax.

straight-line depreciation: A method of depreciation that allows deductions evenly over an asset's useful life.

tax base: Income subject to tax minus allowable deductions.

tax credit: A direct offset against your tax liability.

tax deferral: Income that accumulates tax-free until a taxable event is triggered.

tax exclusion: Income that is never subject to tax.

tax write-off: See "deduction."

taxable income: The income your tax liability is based on.

trade or business: An activity that requires regular and continuous activity as defined by the Internal Revenue Code and case law.

traditional retirement account: A retirement account that allows for a tax deduction of contributions. Earnings grow tax-free and are subject to tax when funds are withdrawn.

useful life: The period over which an asset will be depreciated as specified by the Internal Revenue Code.

wage: Payments to employees for the time they work, usually based on hours.

ACKNOWLEGMENTS

I never thought of myself as a writer. The process was difficult, yet very rewarding. I've been fortunate to have many supporters, especially among my friends and family.

To my mom, Ramona: Thank you for always showing me what hard work and dedication looks like. Even after working long days, she was always willing to read my articles and this book to give me feedback. To my sister Nicole: Thank you for always being there and giving me encouragement during my times of doubt. To my dad, Tim: Thank you for teaching me so many lessons every day as I grew up and instilling a positive mindset that has helped carry me through both the good and bad times that are inevitable in life.

Thank you to all my friends for being more supportive in my endeavors than I could ever imagine. A special thanks to Gina Khawam for taking the time to read and improve this book, and to my friends Billy Ratliff and Katie Becker for always offering words of encouragement and including me in their family.

I wouldn't have accomplished everything I have without the freedom and assistance from all the principals at BeachFleischman, PLLC. From day one, they have given me opportunity and helped me develop relationships that have gotten me to where I am today. To our CEO, Eric Majchzak: Encouraging me to think out-of-the-box and backing me on unconventional ideas has been pivotal. To our COO of Tax, Kim Paskal: You have been an incredible mentor to me.

Your advice has kept me on a great path. To David Cohen: You have showed me the importance of relationships through your actions. To our Director of Marketing, Heather Murray: Helping me realize my vision and creating successful processes has helped both me and the firm achieve better results. Thank you to the rest of the firm for all the collaboration and teamwork that has helped us consistently grow and create the best company culture I could hope for.

It really does take a village: I'm incredibly grateful to be blessed with an amazing real estate team at BeachFleischman, PLLC. I would not be where I am without all their support. Thank you Michael Smith, Ashlea Perron, Doug Shanton, and the rest of the team. Each one of you is always willing to chip in when times are tough, and you've each taught me many lessons over the years.

Relationships are the true measure of wealth. I appreciate all the mentorship and opportunities provided by my many clients. Thank you to Ken McElroy for giving me the ability to say yes to new experiences that have shaped the direction of my career. I admire Ken for his ability to identify great people and surround himself with the best. Thank you Joel Katz for being my unofficial mentor as I invest in real estate and teaching me to always have an exit.

As a new author, I can't even imagine the work it took the KM Press team to bring this book to fruition. Thank you Jennifer Constanza, Marla Markman, Tammy Ditmore, and Peri Gabriel.

INDEX

Note: the letter t following a page number denotes a table.

ABOUT THE AUTHOR

ERIC FREEMAN, CPA, MAcc, is a principal at BeachFleischman PLLC, a top 200 national public accounting firm, and serves as the firm's Real Estate Practice Leader. Eric's expertise is in partnership taxation and complex real estate transactions, including exchanges, mergers, consolidations, buy-outs, cost segregation studies, transaction formation, and qualified opportunity zone funds. Eric also has extensive knowledge in international taxation, hospitality, and high net worth. He has written several articles on real estate taxation that have been featured in *The Trend Report, Phoenix Business Journal,* and numerous other publications. Eric regularly contributes content to multiple YouTube channels, including his own channel, Eric Freeman CPA, and is featured regularly on various podcasts. He offers a unique perspective on real estate taxation from his personal experiences of owning and managing real estate investments, including single-family and multifamily homes, offices, industrial properties, and land. Eric is a graduate of the University of Arizona, where he received a Bachelor of Science in accounting and a Master of Accounting. When he's not working, Eric enjoys snowboarding, poker, hiking, and off-roading.

GET MY FREE MINIGUIDES ON TOPICS LIKE:

- Benefits of Cost Segregation
- Qualifying for Materially Participating Real Estate Professional
- Taxation of Crypto Currencies
- Taking Advantage of the Inflation Reduction Act

Visit EricFreemanCPA.com to download TODAY!

www.ingramcontent.com/pod-product-compliance
Lightning Source LLC
Chambersburg PA
CBHW071204210326
41597CB00016B/1659